Writing the Walls Down

A Convergence of LGBTQ Voices

edited by Helen Klonaris & Amir Rabiyah

trans GENRE
PRESS

Kay Ulanday Barrett ~ Alexis Gumbs
micha cárdenas ~ July Westhale
Ahimsa Timoteo Bodhrán ~ Amal Rana
Eli   Clare   ~   Jerrold   Yam
Hannah J Stein ~ Alfonzo Moret
Rajiv Mohabir ~ Andrea Lambert
Heidi   Andrea   Restrepo   Rhodes
Vivian   Lopez   ~   Dane   Slutzky
librecht baker ~ Margaret Robinson
deborah brandon ~ Celeste Chan
Alex   Simões   ~   Tiffany   Higgins
Sônia Maria Chaves Nepomuceno
Indira Allegra ~ Aiyyana Maracle
Daniel   Chan   ~   Patricia   Powell
Aaron M. Ambrose ~ lee boudakian
Thokozane Minah ~ Jennie Kermode
Ahmunet Jessica Jordon ~ H. Melt
fabian   romero   ~   Joy   Ladin
Trish Salah ~ Nayrouz Abu Hatoum
Vanessa   Huang   ~   Vickie   Vértiz
Amir Rabiyah ~ Helen Klonaris
adrienne maree brown ~ Jordan Rice
TC   Tolbert   ~   Danez   Smith
Janine Mogannam ~ Minal Hajratwala
Moon Flower

Contributors

Writing the Walls Down

A Convergence of LGBTQ Voices

edited by Helen Klonaris & Amir Rabiyah

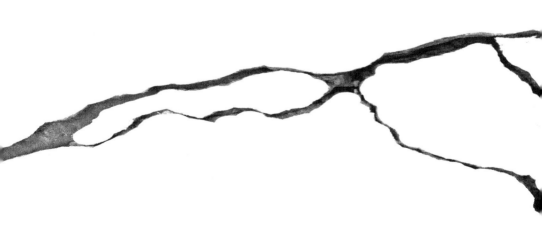

"Grand Design" by Amir Rabiyah originally published in the online journal *Birds Thumb* (Feb. 2014 Vol. 1 Issue 1). birdsthumb.org

"Your Body Burns in Your Room" by Amir Rabiyah originally published on *The Feminist Wire* (Apr. 2014). thefeministwire.com

"Police," "Invincible," "Communion," "Gift," and "Psalm" by Jerrold Yam originally published in *Scattered Vertebrae* (Math Paper Press, 2013).

"We Are The Intersections" by micha cárdenas previously published in *Troubling the Line* (Nightboat Books, 2013) and *Trans Bodies, Trans Selves* (Oxford University Press, 2014).

"Offer the desert, the tower" and "Poem for Abousfian Abdelrazik" by Trish Salah originally published in the chapbook *If a child is a land you may not own.* (Ottawa/Windsor: Flat Singles Press, 2013).

"Our Dangerous Sweetness" by Amir Rabiyah originally published by the online zine: Dangerous Sweetness (July 2012). dangeroussweetness. wordpress.com

In the spirit of *Writing the Walls Down*, the editors have honored the diverse grammatical and stylistic choices of our contributors, and where possible sought to present works in languages other than English.

Published by Trans-Genre Press, August 2015
Los Angeles, CA/Chapel Hill, NC
trans-genre.net

ISBN: 978-0-9851105-9-8
LOC: 2015947924

Cover Photo by Amir Rabiyah
Layout and book design by A.J. Bryce

Anyone who enters here will not feel isolated or alone because this book is an invitation into the heart of the powerful, life-saving word—a crucial place where many of us find our kindred spirit, our blessed haven, our tribe, our home.

-Rigoberto González, author of *Unpeopled Eden*

Contents

Introduction

Helen: Where I come from is an island country off the tip of Florida, north of Cuba and Haiti, west of the West Indies. In that place I was a first generation Greek girl growing up within the larger African Bahamian community, one still grappling with the effects of British colonialism. There were walls I was not supposed to cross: the wall between my house in a middle class neighborhood and the home of my black neighbors next door. The walls between kitchen and the outside world. But I did anyway.

I went weekly to a Greek Orthodox church where the service was in ancient Greek and visitors were rare. When a brown skin woman wandered into this sanctuary, where at the top of the altar, under a large eye, tear-filled, the words "love everyone" watched over us, we set our eyes on her, wondering what she was doing here.

I knew walls. The falling down rock walls people referred to as 'slave walls,' ruins now, along the coast where plantations once upon a time thrived. The walls of Her Majesty's Prison, grey and brown limestone edged across the top with rolls of barbed wire. The walls of the private school I attended, where white parents sent their children after the only other private school on the island let in children of color.

When I arrived in San Francisco in 2005, three years after the falling down of the walls of the World Trade Center, I was running from walls. I had left the church. I had run from a small place where I had come out nationally as a queer woman, where my activism had earned me names like 'witch' and 'militant' and 'angry feminist', rumored death threats, threats of excommunication, a line in an anonymous letter written to me that said "history is strewn with the cadavers of people like you..." I was looking for a place where I might feel something beyond the walls. I thought I could run from walls.

In San Francisco at the age of 35, I fell in love, maybe for the first time. When she kissed me full on the lips in a café on the corner of Guerrero and 19th, and no one looked twice, I thought I had outrun them - those walls. There was so much space for us here.

We were both activists. We met in a laundromat the day Israel began bombing Beirut in 2006. We were both committed to taking down the walls that kept these wars alive. We believed in a world without them. But, as we began to tread deeper into love, every three steps or so, something like a wall would rear up, bruising our knees, our fingers, our lips, our hearts. I thought I knew walls. I thought it was enough to expose them *out there*, talk back to them *out there*. I did not have a language for the ones that showed up invisible, but hard as concrete, between our bodies in bed, between our fingers in the dark of a movie theatre, between our eyes on the platform of a train station as we parted. The ones out there we could name: racism, zionism, colonialism, classism, homophobia, the church, the temple... In here, my own ignorance silenced me. And love, intimacy, hovered, illusive.

Amir: In 2006, Israel was invading Gaza and Lebanon, again. I wasn't eating or sleeping. I kept on looking at IDF maps to see where the latest airstrike was. Did any of my loved ones get hit? Were my friends and my friends' family members still alive? My father and I talked, when the phone lines weren't down. He said, "Don't worry too much; we live in a Christian neighborhood. They are mostly bombing the Muslim neighborhoods." This did not provide me with any relief. People were still dying and being harmed. I was still relatively new to the Bay Area and was just starting to connect with different activists. There were a lot of people coming together in crisis mode to raise awareness about the wars. I wondered why were we able to come together with such intensity in times of crisis, but not as consistently day to day. I felt lonely.

I had just started taking testosterone and was exploring if that was the right step for me in embracing myself as trans. And, it was a difficult and frightening time because I didn't know how or who to talk to about what I was experiencing. I have in my life received multiple kinds of street harassment, usually from police officers and random guys on the street. I felt as though I had to be hypervigilant all the time. I was living in that state constantly. I was afraid of what would happen when I left the house: the homophobic slurs, sexual harassment, beer bottles being thrown at me, tall cis-men leaning in close trying to figure out if I was a man or a woman, threatening me. No place felt safe. And so I did what I could to harden myself, despite being born with incredible sensitivity. I had a hard time knowing when to bring my wall up or down. As a survivor of sexual violence, this also added to my difficulty. Though I worked towards liberation for all peoples, a collective vision of justice outside of myself, it became nearly unfathomable for me to imagine my own body and spirit internalizing and accepting that same spirit of liberation. I recognized this tension within myself, and I recognized it in other members of my community. I kept wondering how was it possible for me to thrive, to know when it was safe to let my guard down, in the midst of ongoing trauma.

Amir and Helen: We met at New College on Valencia Street, before New College became a figment of our imaginations. We had come to write, to earn our MFAs in a place that believed in writing as social activism.

Helen: Amir and I began talking about walls. We were making connections between the walls 'out there' and the walls 'in here'. We began to wonder if the walls out there could really be transformed if we didn't also recognize and transform the ones inside us, between us. Those walls alive and well in our personal unconscious, and in the big and wide collective unconscious where all our stories, all our traumas, all our split off selves, the ones we longed for, the ones we feared, the ones we were ashamed of, the ones we didn't want to recognize, own, claim, the ones we'd abandoned or been forced to abandon long ago; the ones our ancestors had abandoned or been forced to abandon too... all lived on. We wanted to explore these questions. We felt something immense was at stake. Maybe love. Maybe liberation. Maybe our lives on this planet....

Amir: Helen and I began talking. About walls. We were talking about our lovers, our friends, and how so many of us struggled with intimacy and vulnerability. What would it mean for us to be more open with our lovers and our friends? What would it mean to have that love reciprocated? If it came to us, would we hold it close, or would we push it away? What could it mean for us to say yes to such witnessing and love? How could we get there? Were we ready?

Helen: A healer I know says walls are us too. She says when we split off parts of ourselves too dangerous, too shame-filled, too ugly to acknowledge, we make it 'other', we divide it from ourselves and put up a wall. And over time, we forget that what's on the other side of the wall is us too. That the wall is us too.

Amir: Walls are complicated. Some walls are violent and oppressive; such as prison walls and border walls. Some walls are useful and necessary. They can be healthy boundaries and assertions. They can be walls we put up to keep ourselves safe and protect ourselves from harm. I believe as we grow, and if we choose, we may not need the same wall inside of ourselves; we may take one wall down and find another one behind it. It may or may not be still relevant, but our DNA doesn't always know that. Walls don't all look completely the same. There can be walls or barriers between people based on different histories and privileges. I'm interested in all the different ways walls exist, both seen and unseen.

Helen: And soon we wanted to have this conversation in a larger context. We wondered what it would look like to bring together other queer and trans writers, artists, and filmmakers who were exploring these issues as well. So we came up with the idea of a performance.

Amir: We wanted to do a show that would explore the theme of walls through the arts. We were accepted to be a part of the National Queer Arts Festival in 2011, and we were very excited. Our years of conversation and dialogue were finally culminating into a performance that we could share with the Bay Area community. At the time of the planning of the performance, my health was continuing to decline, and I was still struggling with debt and being broke. I wanted to write a piece that explored my relationship to my disability, as well as disability within my own family. I wanted it to be a piece that exposed the struggle, beauty, and pain of living with disabilities. I wanted to explore my experience growing up in a mixed-race and mixed-class family. As I worked on this narrative piece, the submissions began coming in. It was incredible to look over all of the videos, performance pieces, music, and stories that artists were submitting. It was incredible to feel more connected to other artists, whose work was also speaking to many of the questions Helen and I had been asking ourselves over the years.

Helen and Amir: In 2011 we debuted The Walls Project at the National Queer Arts Festival in San Francisco and knew that even after we had completed that project, our exploration, our dialogue together and with other queer artists was not over. The idea of an anthology was coalescing and by 2013 it had become insistent.

Helen: I was unemployed and wrestling with the tensions of being in a relationship where there was an imbalance of financial resources. Again, it was easy to look outside myself at that imbalance and determine the walls out there were to blame for my difficulty in sustaining myself. I only needed to look out my car window at the Occupy protests, the monumental divides between the one percent and everyone else, to see very real walls setting us apart from each other. But I was curious about how those walls also existed inside of me. Which part of me had I relegated to living just above the poverty line, and which part of me was the one percent?

Amir and Helen: Exploring these questions of walls in an anthology that brought together a wide gathering of trans and queer writers from many different cultures, countries, and communities seemed powerful. And we didn't want to focus solely on how walls separate us, or divide us from ourselves, but also how they connect us, and how they can become opportunities for dialogue and healing. We wanted art and stories to share testimonies of resistance and transformation. We wanted art and stories that portrayed power and privilege with complexity and nuance.

Both of us had been influenced deeply by the important work of writers and the anthologies they produced, and we wanted to contribute to this truth-telling tradition. Anthologies like *Food For Our Grandmothers: Writings by Arab-American,* and *Arab-Canadian Feminists* edited by Jo Kadi, and *This Bridge Called My Back*, edited by Cherríe Moraga and Gloria E. Anzaldúa were watershed events for us, shifting our consciousness and creating new space for what was possible; *Colonize This: Young Women of Color on Today's Feminism*, edited by Daisy Hernández and Bushra Rehman, as well as *Our Caribbean: A Gathering of Lesbian and Gay Writings from the Antilles*, edited by Thomas Glave, widened those spaces even further.

Amir: For both of us also, it was important to make sure that this anthology represented a culturally diverse spectrum of LGBTQ people. We wanted to make sure that LGBTQ people of color's voices were centered. We are happy to say that the majority of our submissions were from people of color, and the majority of the artists in the anthology are people of color.

Helen: I have no doubt that our lives as two-spirit people, queers, transgender people, and LGBTQ people, are at stake, and that our grappling in poetry, story, essay, and visual art in these pages is crucial to our survival in our imaginations and in the world. I also think that our grappling with/in these walls, our transformation of them, has the power to transform walls beyond our own lives. In the small place I come from there is no 'queer agenda;' there can be no single issue agenda because the lives of LGBTQ people are not separate from, are integrally connected to, the lives of heterosexuals and cisgender people as well. It is my hope that the medicine, the prayer, the ceremony, the revelation, and the healing in these pages will be adaptogenic; that is, will go wherever they are needed most.

Helen and Amir: This anthology came out of an alchemy that has always existed between us as well as a friendship that has always felt honoring and sacred. Working together as co-editors has only deepened our friendship. And that friendship has been a catalyst for the creative process and journey of this book. The work that came to us as submissions, crafted so tenaciously, tenderly, with vulnerability, out of the visceral experiences of the artists' lives, has an alchemy of its own. There were countless times that the words and images on the page made us weep, deepened our perspectives, jolted us out of convenient perceptions of identities, and widened the possibilities that existed for us, and for being in world. The process of reading, editing, and putting together this book has put us in a continual state of transformation. The journey has been an honor and a blessing.

Finally, *Writing the Walls Down* would not have been possible without the vision of A.J. Bryce of Trans-Genre Press. In October of 2013, we sent out a handful of query letters to independent presses. We held our breath. Days later, we received a beautiful response from A.J. expressing his excitement and interest in our project. Soon after, all three of us spoke on Skype, and we felt a connection to A.J. As we talked, it became clear that A.J. was deeply invested in supporting the communities he was a part of. He has believed in this anthology from the beginning, and we have appreciated his heart, his dedication, and his unwavering commitment.

We welcome you, reader, to our anthology. Gather with the artists and writers contained in the pages of this book; hear our stories, cries, desperation, rawness, beauty, struggle, and courage, and join us in a call of unapologetic celebration. Here is what we envision: as you read, you too will become part of the convergence at the walls; in this space of words, of spirit, of heart, of the tenacity of our bodies, we believe in the possibility of what we are creating together: our presence at these walls changes them.

To all who live behind walls.
To all who travel between them.

Alexis Gumbs

an element of radical waywardness[1]

there was always the one. that walked the dirt path crooked infringing on the grass. that cleared the forest in some adinkra design that for sure could only be seen from heaven. that wore out the outside of one shoe and the inside of the other from their everyday crooked tendencies. the one that danced, planted, plotted, and eventually drove as if he was falling down, as if his ear loved the ground, as if he was suspended from above by a lazy god he loved enough to keep believing in.

there was one. every village, every small town, eventually every zip code had one. and needed that one so they could measure their straightness, ninety degree their angles, perpendicular their walks. you know, relief. but then something happened and the sideways dancers, dirt path deviators, asymptote tracers started to lean towards each other more and more and they found each other on corners stunned and grateful to have people who could look into their diagonal eyes, their own people with no desire to adjust their half-cocked hats. they found each other and they reshaped the streets together with their feet tending to tiltsphere.

and the townships who had lost their tilters questioned their own straightness, shaped themselves to questions, curved in other ways. they didn't think to wish that their crooked fools had stayed, they just looked up to the sky and asked and listened to the ground and didn't realize that their angles grew acutely towards the sound of walking sideways and they

1 Hortense Spillers "Formalism Comes to Harlem," in *Black White and In Color*, 81.

found themselves leaving town down the same routes that had erstwhile always led them home. they roamed out of earshot of the talking drums and bells that had forever held them well and they found music that made them doubt and made them jump and tilt and shout. they found each other.

and then the tilting magic spread like a lightness in the head, an orientation towards the dead while we're still living. and our streets became forgiving and our buildings became round we gave up straightness and guess what? nothing at all was missing.

Ahimsa Timoteo Bodhrán

Sage

In each place,
purple flowers, fuzzed tongue,
fragrance felt, rubbed, lifted to fingers,
nose, nostrils, inhaled in, no other
smell left possible. An overwhelming
of senses. Wood chip, dirt, stump
to sit on, clearing in the round,
each four, water on rock,
sizzle. Steam. Some of thin leaf, others
round, pointed, a different way to collect
water (counter-counter-clock-wise), bring
it to root, hopefully still
in soil. Dried for home
cleansing, each foot lifted,
then down the back, before
entering, a gradient of genders, each
place a space for us, left on altar
for after bad visit, magick, time
for battle/war, our aim a good one, no
bowl or rug, basket, for the wall, used daily,
before entering, leaving,
the breaking of ties, new love,
house
warming with sweat, peek of night sky,
stars, or day sun, warming rocks
fire, and the flap
closes again; we are here within
this womb. Each time we leave,
we are born again, medicine

deep within us, prayers,
songs, in memory, Mother on our
feet and faces. No Christian
saviour greets us at the door.
Our Ancestors are the ground
beneath us.

Vanessa Huang

Gaza song
for S

made of nightfall chimes

carried by wind's knowing sigh

sounds from a childhood music

box I no longer remember

dancing legacy of Creek and Cherokee stewards

meeting footstep vibration of courage broken

and recovered, seas and lands

away moving and chanting in strong purpose

still believing in life

electric and living

with room to grow old without horror

stars of light

crossing Rafah to tend to Gazans hit by

Israeli sunrise shellings

each broken heart

breathing in prayer to simply live

and love

each desperate inhalation through pillars of smoke

remembering to keep steady through constant groundshake

and the still relentless laughter of evil. I am terrified

to look at another image of sky breaking

open the living

room of someone's home the rockets'

fire and digital world were not invited into.

This is not a ribbon dance: This is a photograph

of terror I've tried and tried to not reproduce

with my words, and I want to share

now of these menacing strings of fire

a festival of lights

grotesquely frozen in time

before they continue to streak down

and down

splintering the middle of a square, behind the basketball hoop

as people bolt under the building.

I reconnect with your songstress

winter within winter

and I hunger for growing blankets of outrage and warmth

to Gaza

and Palestine

and Syria

and Rikers

and every living and enduring spirit contained and caught

in unnatural seas of fire

and the experience of lockup by lines drawn in greed

onto this precious grieving land beneath our swollen feet.

I wish for healing across

generations of bone-broken limbs

and courage-broken hearts

through silence and scream

the teachings of elders stolen

across land and sea.

I wish for this healing:

honest

true

full and wide

enough to cover the sun

endlessly reflected in sea's unerring mirror.

I wish for you and I the stories woven

in cloth from our grandmothers' grandmothers' grandmothers

I wish for the exchange of honest feelings

living rooms full of laughter and transformation

I wish for dances passed through blood

recipes written in our bones

and kitchens full of the family spices

we thirst for to carry us home.

East Point, GA
November 19, 2012

Written in call and response with the poetry of June Jordan ("Moving Towards Home"), Suheir Hammad ("Gaza"), Mohja Kahf ("Syria Boxes"), and Rafeef Ziadah ("We teach life, sir").

"relentless laughter of evil" borrowed from June Jordan. "a festival of lights" and "winter within winter" borrowed from Suheir Hammad. "to cover the sun" borrowed from Rafeef Ziadah.

Amal Rana

when the skies were free

when the skies were still free
we shimmered
humming birds melting into each other
earth bleeding music into a lover's mouth

when the skies were still free
we never stepped sideways out of fear
before entering a masjid
never wondered if walls
had informant ears
if the imam or the person praying next to us
was working for the fbi
we never paused in the middle of a walk
you told me about a new islamic centre
hope vibrating in your voice at the thought
of finally finding community
until i deflated your excitement with homeland security truths
meant to make our lives feel like a lie
spilled unwilling warnings about entrapment, detention,
deportation
fahad hashmi, aafia siddiqui, ehsanul sadequee
guantanamo, bagram
hunger strikes
force feedings
solitary confinements
words pushing out of me
becoming concrete
cutting off the open air around you
brick by brick

layers of fear spread thick in between
to cover any cracks
that might let in spring days
and the uncurling of cherry blossoms and hope

when the skies were still free
our spirits walked for miles
hand in hand
no walls of fear
hemming us in
keeping each other out
eyes full of stars instead of impossibility
your heart still beating
in tandem with mine
before borders stopped its rhythm
tried to swallow you whole
deemed you criminal
for daring to breathe while being muslim

when the skies are again free
we will meet on a path laid with pink petals
rain falling in fragrant buds all around us
we will shimmer
humming birds melting into each other
earth bleeding music into a lover's mouth

Amir Rabiyah

Grand Design
(for M81 and the rest of us)

today collect the dazzling shelter of flowers
stitch a crown large enough for the globe
fragrant enough for satellites to lift their noses
take the prayer of night into your arms
as she sleeps, breathe with her
breathe with the night
there are times when there is nothing
left to do, but create
form the unseen into a tangible communion
of stardust, place the galaxy on your tongue
let your mouth be a wondrous glow
your words a beacon
when everything is lost
imagine yourself as more than an earth-
quaking body a gift
the streaking tail of a comet
become that which holds your eye
that which makes you gasp

Amir Rabiyah

doctors make forceps with their fingers. they imitate the smallestviolin.yourpainisnotanotebutawhine.youhavecome to know how they cope when confronted with the unknown. the oxycodone numbs 1/4 of your thumb, but leaves you swimming in your bath. splashing, convinced you are a rubber ducky. you laugh when you are alone. your voice is a stranger and a friend.

Your Body Burns In Your Room

you salute the landscape from the square acre of bed

as for the peeled wallpaper: it's a rolling wave,

a leaf curling, anything, but the fetal position,

it's a bastion of ribbons in your hair,

it's a smoke signal formed from a sciatic spark

rising to your ceiling, forming itself into

a genderless God. It's the miracle you can't undo,

the waking up even when you don't want to,

how you create from rock bottom, the dirt under

your nails, the half moons, the scars in the night sky

Andrea Lambert

Invocation

I.

Ava Maria Madre de Dios
Ava Maria Madre de Dios
Ava Maria
I know not the prayer
Ava Janet
This one's for you

I know you sit there in the old folks' home
Listening to the radio
To the words of Howard Stern

I am endlessly thankful for the carved four-post solid
The dresser with the glacial oculus
Enough drawers for me
My ex,
And my future.
For the two matched chairs
One lent to my baldheaded roommate
To show her welcome.
The table that holds my record player
Where I play Pearl Bailey and Johnny Mathis
For so much I thank you
For the set of cocktail glasses
For wine, water and guava juice
With copper and teal sailing ships
For the silverware with rosebuds
All these accouterments that give luxury to my

Otherwise spare rooms
I thank you
Grandma Janet
Grandpa Dewey.
For the gifts
From you come my genes

I was there
When you gave your house up
When you went to the home
When you died.

II.

I am the mass of my mothers and fathers.
Virginia and Gary and Janet and Dewey

You know not what you did.

You fell in love.

Begninia and Guido
You wanted to be Americans
You became Virginia
The beauty of El Cajon
You became Gary
The soldier in WWII
You never knew the burden of what you carried
You changed your names
You fell in love

And I don't blame you

Begninia
Virginia
My abuela

I always wanted to be as beautiful as your pictures

I didn't know the cursed nature of pretty
I love you as the strength behind my family
I know your brother killed a man
I know your sister was schizophrenic
I know your brother died on a motorcycle

I don't want to be alone anymore
I drink from these glasses
Sleep on this bed.
Night after night
I think of you

III.

Janet
You wore pink to his funeral
Dewey went after you with a butcher knife.
Dewey thought you were cheating
Dewey gave me everything for Christmas
Dewey who I never suspected
Dewey of the beer belly and pink blue eyes
Dewey of the dishonorable discharge
And faded letters from a man in Kentucky

Janet and Dewey of the Queen Anne furniture.
In which you never sat,
Inherited from an aunt
That Dewey may have slept with
We'll never know
And death is quiet and peaceful enough for forgiveness

IV.

All I know.
Behind my pills
Is I'm bipolar and psychotic
A mix from all of you
Whom I love

Despite
Whatever
You've granted me.
I mean not the heirlooms
However lovely
I mean
More, the bed is haunted.

Sleeping in Virginia's bed
Christmas post Gary's death
I popped some beers
Fell asleep with Reader's Digest
I sensed a man
Knew it was you
Gary looking for Virginia and finding me
Me
Twenty-nine and tipsy in her blue flannel nightie
I ache for grandma to hear you
Remembering your yellowed body
Your cold hand when I went in late
I wept at your funeral in a black mantilla
I hoped now whatever I could give you would be enough.
I always loved you
For teaching me of Sicily

I feel your spirit which I had sensed
walking the halls many times
I feel your spirit looking past me for Virginia
I try to speak with you
You spent the night in my dream.
I hope to be close enough to Virginia
And give you what you need

My heart aches for both of you.

V.

It is different with Dewey.

Dewey never came back to see me,
His death is different.
He left me with the blood
Blessed and cursed.
The madness scores me
The liturgy of pills that I take each dawn and evening
The penance of AA
The catechism of psychiatry
My genes, I know that pain I stalk it with my boyfriends
As you have
As you did
As you tried to kill Janet
As Tod laid his hands around my neck

"Do you want to die, Andrea?"
"Do you want me to take you to the river?"

I do not want to die
I want to live

The grim echoes of the schizophrenia
That I felt taking me to all the hospitals
And out again to lead and live in spirit
To be psychic
To be queer
To be mad
To be fiery

To have white trash sass

My madness I feel from him,
My paranoia

As the child of this violence
All I did was drug myself:

Cocaine
Speed

Heroin
Meth
Adderall
Xanax
Seroquel
Depakote
Risperdal
Wellbutrin
Abilify
Lexapro
Topamax
Tegretol
Haldol
Ativan
Klonopin
Prozac
Saphris
Marijuana
How much will be enough?
How much medicine will be enough?

To end this night
To find me peace
For how many nights will I sleep on the bed of our madness?

Burning

Before

The phoenix rises

Margaret Robinson

Standing in the Intersection:
Aboriginality, Poverty, & Mental Health

I find it difficult to write about myself. It makes me feel vulnerable, raw, and overexposed. I'm more comfortable writing in the abstract. I'm more comfortable with theory, with statistics. But some experiences are personal and perhaps are understood best through story.

I am a member of Generation X, a third wave feminist, an academic, a bisexual activist, and a researcher in the field of LGBTQ mental health. Being involved in activism was probably inevitable for me. Growing up, the power of human action—for good or bad—was continually displayed on television. The year I turned sixteen I watched the Berlin Wall fall, tanks roll over students in Tiananmen Square, the *Exxon Valdez* crash, and the outpouring of grief and anger in the wake of the Montreal Massacre. The world has never felt like a safe place to me. My first sexual education class included a discussion about AIDS. When I enter a room for the first time I note the exits and I plan what I will do in the event of gunfire. Yet I've also seen remarkable progress. The year I came out as bisexual the World Health Organization finally declassified "homosexuality" as a disease, Nelson Mandela was freed from prison, and the world wide web was invented. I know people can change the world because I've watched it happen.

As I enter my forties I've begun to reflect on the paths that I've walked in life. I realize that I stand in the middle of an intersection: my Aboriginality, my class, and my mental health. All three have shaped the person I am today—perhaps most of all in those moments when my identities meet and blend.

Aboriginality

I'm a Mi'kmaw woman. My ancestors lived on the east coast of North America, in what are now Maine, New Brunswick, Nova Scotia, Prince Edward Island, and Newfoundland. I am descended from those who survived when our Mi'kmaq population shrunk from 50,000 to 1800 under intentional genocidal strategies such as starvation, typhus, and smallpox infection. My grandmother grew up on the Lennox Island Reserve in the province of Prince Edward Island. As a child she and her sister were sent to a Catholic school where they were beaten for speaking Mi'kmaq. For decades my grandmother denied her Aboriginal identity, afraid of the stigma it would bring on her family. By the time I was born, in 1973, nobody in my family spoke Mi'kmaq. Our family is no exception; only a third of children attending reserve schools in the province of Nova Scotia speak Mi'kmaq as their first language. I learned about my ancestors in school, as a brief unit in Canadian history. I was in my thirties before I read anything that portrayed my people in a positive light, focusing on our democracy, our values, and our resilience.

As I get older I've become more aware of what generations of government-mandated assimilation have taken from me. My white mother has spent more time on the Rez than I have. I remember the first time I attended an event at a native center in Toronto.

Standing in a circle with the other participants, I realize I am the only woman wearing pants—already I am doing things wrong. The elder leads an opening prayer in a language I do not know. I listen intently, unsuccessfully trying to identify a verb or noun. I have studied French, German, Latin, and Ancient Greek, but none of these colonial languages help me now. A woman walks around the circle holding a seashell, fanning smoldering sage and sweetgrass, offering us the opportunity to purify ourselves in the smoke. I know the ceremony is called "smudging," but I don't yet know its meaning. Ignorant of the protocols of the ceremony, I copy what the people before me do—scooping the smoke with my hands and moving it over my head, chest, and feet. The scent immediately conjures memories of my grandmother's home, yet I never saw her smudge. "Is this something she did in secret?" I wonder. Everyone before me says "Miigwetch," so I say it too. I later learn that it means "thank you." At that point I know more Ojibwe than I know Mi'kmaq.

Despite the losses of colonialism and assimilation, I've also been fortunate. I know my Mi'kmaq name. Growing up rural, I experienced the ties with nature that our traditions take as a given, but which many urban Aboriginals have been denied. I learned quillwork from my father, and I got to witness my parents take an active role in Native politics.

I enter a period of reclamation. Using an online dictionary, I learn to introduce myself in Mi'kmaq. I Google the meaning of the ceremonies in which I participate to learn what they mean (although I have to wade through a sea of new age appropriation to do so). I learn to offer tobacco and request advice from an elder. I've made friends who possess more cultural knowledge than I have. These mentors answer my ignorant questions with good humour and generosity, and they support me as I work through my anger at colonialism, racism, and a litany of historical injustices.

As a woman with white skin privilege, I don't look the way we've been trained to expect Aboriginal people to look. Despite my dark hair, almond eyes, and high cheekbones, I am rarely recognized as an Aboriginal person, and I must constantly out myself, even to those most like me. As a bisexual, I can see the parallel. Sitting as I often do now, in conference and meeting rooms filled with other Aboriginal people, many of whom know me and know my work on two-spirited mental health, I finally feel visible, seen for who and what I am. It feels like a kind of home. A kind of family.

The more I learn about Aboriginal cultures the more I see them reflected in what I once thought were simply my family's eccentricities—our matriarchal power structure, our childrearing habits, and our attitude toward the police. Those of us who grew up without Indian status sometimes struggle with feelings of inauthenticity, as if the Federal government's refusal to grant us Indian status reflects some failure within ourselves. Yet I now realize that our family traditions are no less Native for being off the Rez.

Poverty

I grew up in rural poverty. For most of my childhood we lived in a two-room shack my father built using carpentry skills he'd learned in prison. In many respects, rural poverty has changed remarkably little over the past two hundred years. In the winter we melted snow on the wood stove, picking out the evergreen needles so we could bathe. We transported our fresh drinking water from a stream that emptied into a ditch by the side of the road. Our bathroom was sometimes an outhouse, sometimes a bucket hidden behind a discreet woolen curtain. In school, when we read *Little House In The Big Woods* by Laura Ingalls Wilder, I wondered if I was the only person in class for whom the story didn't feel like fiction. I was in my teens before our house had a working toilet. I still remember the joy I felt as we huddled around it, flushing it again and again, watching the water swirl away.

More than anything, being poor was about constant humiliation. Once, my parents needed to travel the few miles to town so we began to hitchhike. Although I couldn't have been more than five, I was too embarrassed to mimic my parents by putting out my thumb to ask for a ride. Worse than not having the proper clothes, school supplies, or the popular toys were the questions from my peers as to *why* I lacked these things.

The message that poverty is a personal failing is everywhere in our society. The marks of my poverty became marks of personal inadequacy, so I learned to hide them from others. I never invited friends over. I became fastidious about my appearance. I gave myself less leeway in my social behavior, feeling pressure to seem respectable. To feel normal. I dreamed of new clothes, of brand-name toys, of carpeted rooms with wallpaper and polished furniture. But more than middle class possessions, I dreamed of middle class respectability. I became a chameleon, mimicking middle class manners, values, and dress. I dropped my accent. I lied about what my parents did for a living.

My parents had grown up in urban poverty in the 1940s, amidst lice, bedbugs, and violence. Student loans afforded me a way out of the cycle of poverty. Attending university while poor was a strange experience. I worked minimum wage jobs in secret, since as graduate students we technically weren't allowed to work. Using the university food bank was such a humiliating experience that I never returned. A guard at the door demanded we provide bank statements and pay stubs. As if anyone would run such a gauntlet of shame if they had any other choice. I bought groceries and paid my rent with cash advances on my credit card instead. Mastercard didn't judge me.

Professors assumed that everyone in the classroom was middle class or above, that our parents were paying our tuition, and that poverty and class distinctions would be understood theoretically, not viscerally. The message was clear: poor people are things we study. I felt alienated by writings that framed working class identity around well-paying union jobs in the manufacturing industry. My class experience was of chronic unemployment, of dying resource extraction industries such as fishing and logging, and of criminalized activities like bootlegging, drug selling, or kiting cheques. Being closeted about my poverty meant that people speaking on behalf of the "voiceless" poor dominated the conversation. We watched Powerpoint slides revealing the squalor of Aboriginal reserves. The images were meant to illicit pity, but felt familiar, even comforting to me. Although materially deprived, my childhood had been happy, my parents kind, loving, and supportive. The few times I did reference my own poverty in class people were quick to dismiss my experience as a false consciousness or an appropriation. We were being taught to focus on our privileges.

Being broke shaped my ability to participate in LGBTQ culture. I attended discussion and activism groups in part because they were free, but going out for drinks afterwards, or attending a dance was often impossible. Many LGBTQ community events offer a sliding scale, but taking advantage of such benefits requires that we out ourselves as poor. Already marginalized in queer community as Aboriginal and as bisexual, I didn't want to risk exposing myself to more shame and stigma. Organizing events at least got me free admission.

Poverty also made dating difficult. There were the obvious issues of affording the price of a movie ticket, or lacking something "nice" to wear. But it was the clash in values that was most jarring. Middle class partners spent money with a quiet confidence that there would always be more coming in. Their assurances that any current financial crisis would "work itself out" was infuriating yet absurdly funny. In my world, things didn't work themselves out. I had to do it myself.

Being poor was also out of sync with the queer agenda of the time, which focused on middle class gay and lesbian families, equal marriage rights, and the power of the pink dollar. Poor queers were bad for the cause. Once, after months of volunteer work with a queer organization, I had to cancel a workshop I had planned to give because my new employer required that I work that evening. The leader of the queer group exploded in anger at me when I called to explain. She called me irresponsible, unreliable, and implied that if I were a lesbian instead of a bisexual woman, I would have better priorities. It hurt dreadfully, but looking back, I can't blame her for her anger. She didn't know that I'd been unemployed for over a year and was now collecting welfare. She didn't know that I counted myself lucky to have finally found work, even if it paid less than minimum wage by framing itself as a training program. She didn't know because I was too ashamed to tell her.

Although I've moved out of poverty I'm never entirely free of it. My values have been shaped by the experience of scarcity and the fear of judgment. Poverty marks my body as well as my mind. I've lost 5 of my adult teeth—one because an extraction was cheaper than filling the cavities. I have bone degeneration in my skull. I feel a jolt of panic when the phone rings or I hear the doorbell. The arrival of mail elicits a gnawing in the pit of my stomach. And I have intense periods of depression.

Depression

Initially, I didn't understand what was going on when I became depressed. Sometimes the world just seemed overwhelmingly horrible, my relationships pointless, the future bleak and hopeless. These periods lasted a few days, weeks, or sometimes months. When I was down I rarely left the house, showered, or spoke to anyone. I was overwhelmingly angry one moment, crying in the fetal position the next. I slept for 15 hours or more at a time. My weight ballooned until none of my clothes fit and I couldn't leave the house. I became afraid to interact with people, developing crippling social anxiety. I once left a store without the food I'd come for because a sales clerk said hello to me.

I constantly worried that I would commit some sudden violent or self-destructive act. Studying for my Master's degree I had a depression so severe that I moved heavy furniture in front of my balcony door to prevent myself from jumping. Since I have an aunt who committed suicide I take those impulses very seriously. I started charting my moods and keeping a journal. I discovered that my depressions were cyclical and began to plan ahead. Knowing that my depressions were temporary made a world of difference. Until then, I thought that my perception of the world during my depressions was accurate rather than seeing it as distorted by stress.

Depression does not occur in isolation. My work in LGBTQ mental health has helped me to see my health and that of my family and my communities in perspective. Mental illness is a product of social forces acting on our bodies. Research shows that in self-governing Aboriginal communities, for example, where people had access to their culture, suicide rates dropped to near zero. By contrast, Aboriginal communities with little autonomy, under heavy pressure to assimilate, saw suicide rates skyrocket. Chronic unemployment, poverty, racism, colonialism, homophobia, biphobia or transphobia increases the production of cortisol in our brain—the chemical that regulates our feelings of stress. Too much cortisol causes weight gain, lethargy, anxiety, depression, insomnia, damages bone growth, lowers our immune system, and causes problems with memory and attention. Growing up poor left me and other members of my family vulnerable to depression, anxiety and thoughts of suicide, sick, exhausted, struggling to control our weight, and more likely to have problems in school. Negative stereotypes blame the poor themselves for what are actually the effects of poverty. Even today, despite having earned a PhD, I struggle with the stereotype that I am lazy and stupid. I am afraid to be seen taking a break.

Mental illness often separates us from the very social support that has been shown to keep us healthy. At the hospital where I work there is a wall built by former patients of what was then called the Provincial Lunatic Asylum. The wall once circled the hospital, cutting the asylum off from the city outside. Although only a small piece of the wall remains as a heritage structure, the metaphorical walls that separate those of us with mental illness or neurological differences from those deemed "normal" or "healthy" are still solidly established. The stigma of mental illness in LGBTQ communities makes it difficult for us to ask for or receive support. I have lost too many friends to suicide. Many members of our LGBTQ communities still harbor fears that recognizing depression, anxiety, or similar problems will reinforce the idea that our sexual or gender identities are themselves a type of sickness. Personally, I have found more power in claiming my struggles and in identifying their social and political roots.

Intersecting Identity

Being out as bisexual mixes with my Aboriginal identity and my poverty history in dangerous ways. Native women are stereotyped as promiscuous and self-destructive, exposing us to greater sexual violence and making it difficult if not impossible to get justice when we are attacked. Since 1980, over 500 native women have gone missing or been found murdered in Canada. Most of these disappearances are unsolved and uninvestigated. In addition to coping with the trauma of experiences such as residential schools, the Sixties Scoop of native children from their families and their forced adoption into White homes, and the psychological effects of cultural genocide, Aboriginal women struggle daily with the knowledge that our lives are not valued.

Likewise, when I come out as bisexual I am characterized as insatiable, promiscuous, diseased, and treacherous. I once had a personals ad rejected because I had used the word bisexual. Angry, on the phone with their head office in Texas, an apologetic gay man explained that while the words "gay" and "lesbian" were acceptable, identifying myself as bisexual implied that I was looking for a threesome. Coming out to my family, my mother told me I was "oversexed." Bisexual women report the highest rates of sexual and intimate partner violence, in large part as a result of these stereotypes. Those of us who are labeled and psychiatrized are additionally vulnerable, not only to being sexually and violently assaulted, but to being dismissed as delusional, attention-seeking, or deserving of such treatment.

Finally, to be poor is to be stereotyped as dirty, immoral, and sexually wanton. The "welfare queen" is both racialized as non-white and framed as promiscuous, outside the respectability of the middle class family unit. Aboriginal people have been living in poverty for so long that being poor has come to be seen as part of our culture, with Aboriginal restaurants serving "traditional" food such as canned meat. I have never been so visible as an Aboriginal woman as when I was also visible as poor. To be a poor, Aboriginal, bisexual woman with a mental illness is a perfect storm of vulnerability.

Yet the intersections are also points where activism overlaps and solidarity ignites. I've been involved in queer activism and bisexual community building for over 20 years. Activism gave me a door into queer belonging, enabling me to bond with gay, lesbian, and trans colleagues, and produced my strongest friendships. Activism has also been a doorway to solidarity with other Aboriginal people and our settler allies. Thanks to movements such as Idle No More, issues facing Aboriginal people in North America have never been more visible. There is a spirit of rebellion, of strength, and a desire for change that hasn't been seen in North America since the rise of the American Indian Movement in the late 1960s. The solidarity and the politics of the movements in which I participate are a source of support and wellness for me. My experience as an Aboriginal woman, as a bisexual woman who has experienced poverty, and who walks with depression has informed my activism and my academic work in ways that keep me grounded. Access to culturally safe, competent, affordable, and accessible health service is not an abstract issue for me. Such issues are at once personal and political—a source of strength, pride, and vision. While I still walk on a number of paths, I'm finally optimistic about where these paths are going.

Eli Clare

Might the Walls Begin Again

I ride the slow loops of history and memory back, each faint arc shimmering. Back and back to my first glimmer. Here. Here: *white coats, voices, a table, fear of falling.*

It's 1966, and I am two-and-a-half, just beginning to walk, no longer stumping around on my knees but balancing on my own two feet. Not yet talking, not a single spoken word, but using a sign language of my own creation.

It's 1966, and my parents have brought me for diagnostic testing to the Fairview Hospital and Training Center, which at its opening in 1908 was known as the State Institution for the Feeble-Minded.

> *shadows cast on walls painted pink*
> *green eggshell blue but*
> *dingy, festooned with rules*

It's 1966, and they give me an IQ test. American eugenicist Henry Goddard developed that test in the early 1910s, wanting to quantify who was a *moron* and who not. He tried it out first at Ellis Island, declaring huge numbers of Jewish, eastern European, and Italian immigrants morons, defects, and therefore ineligible for entry into the US.

It's 1966, and Fairview houses nearly 3,000 people. In 1920, the residents were diagnosed *idiot* and *imbecile*; in 1950, *retarded* and *handicapped*; and now they are beginning to be called *developmentally disabled*, not yet known as *intellectually disabled*. The diagnostic language slips and slides over the decades. Many of these 3,000 people have lived here, locked away, for their entire lives.

It's 1966, and I score badly on their tests. Not many years before, they would have declared me a *low grade moron* or a *high grade imbecile*, but by the '60s the words have changed, although neither the laws nor institutions have, and so I become *mentally retarded*.

> *walls festooned with rules*
> *soaked in urine and fear*
> *built of brick and mortar*

It's 1966, and Oregon doctors still sterilize folks on a monthly basis. They use Oregon's eugenics law, first passed in 1917, to justify involuntary castrations, vasectomies, hysterectomies, tubal ligations—2,648 in total by the time the law is repealed in 1983.

It's 1966, and I join the ranks of those targeted. The Oregon law names us "feeble-minded, insane, epileptics, habitual criminals, moral degenerates, and sexual perverts, who are persons potential to producing offspring who, because of inheritance of inferior or antisocial traits, would probably become a social menace...." Sterilization is often the sole criteria for release from Fairview.

If my parents did nothing else, they didn't leave me there. They certainly could have.

> *walls built of brick and mortar,*
> *2x4 and plywood, plaster and*
> *chicken wire, self splits from self*

Historian Phil Ferguson writes: "Fairview... was not the first such institution to open or the last to close. Even at its peak population, it was not the biggest. As those who lived there know only too well, it definitely was not the best, but as others who lived elsewhere can also testify, it certainly was not the worst...."

If there can be such a thing, Fairview... could be called a 'typical' institution for people with developmental disabilities."

10,000 people lived there over the course of 92 years. Sisters, fathers, cousins, mothers, uncles went missing from their home communities, turned into case files.

I watch a film made by a man whose younger sister disappeared. Jeff Daly was six years old, Molly two, when she simply vanished— not even a shadow or secret to mark her departure, just a sudden unexplained absence as if she had never existed.

> *self splits from self, abandons*
> *skin heart bone*
> *vanishes into the walls*

In *Where's Molly?* Jeff documents his search, tracking Molly's disappearance from a note found in his father's wallet to a case file complete with photos—easily mistaken for mug shots—to Fairview.

Along the way, he finds a 1959 promotional film made by Fairview called *In Our Care*. The grainy black and white footage crackles and pops. He first sees Molly here as she sits on the floor of a crowded bare room, playing with a ball. She looks straight into the camera—eyes crooked, ready, still inquisitive; unlike her later mug shots, defiant and shuttered.

We see nurses tending children in cribs, row upon row in room after room. We see a cafeteria where a chaos of children eat; a laundry room where women fold sheets, men tend big steam dryers. We see a woman in an isolation cage.

> vanishes into the walls, the dark
> breathing spaces between 2x4s
> gaps in mortar and brick, a refuge

We don't see the cow whips, handcuffs, head cages, razor straps, straitjackets, the scalding water and cold water punishments, the threats of acid baths, the realities of rape. I contemplate what it means to describe Fairview as "not the best, but... certainly... not the worst."

In 1966, did my parents drive to Fairview in search not only of a diagnosis but also a potential place to leave me? Were they fed lies and platitudes about custodial care for their eldest crippled child? I imagine my parents watching *In Our Care*, absorbing the narrator's cheerful authority into their bodies; relief, love, shame vying for attention.

Decades of confinement, boredom, punishment, psych meds; hard labor in the kitchen, laundry, farm, dairy—I came close, so close. My escape, yet another ghost.

a dark breathing refuge
the walls become home
shiver and groan

My only glimmer: *white coats loom, voices, a cold, cold table, fear of falling, body tumbling to the floor, out of control, not mine.*

And after Fairview closed in 2000, arsonists, graffiti artists, bulldozers all arrived to make their mark on those abandoned buildings.

When a prison, asylum, army depot closes, what do we do with the bricks, land, gravestones? What happens to the stories, poems, unadulterated pain? When we tear down the walls, what do they release, and what do they take with them?

the walls shiver and groan
might they begin again
become a trellis

I want to know all their names—every single person locked away at Fairview over the course of those 92 years, a list of 10,000. Where did they stash their sorrow and rage; what small pleasures did they steal? They could be a demolition brigade armed with sledgehammers.

a trellis covered
with morning glories

Jordan Rice

Tresses

My father rings our apple trees with his own urine,
says the scent will scare off starving deer which strip

his low limbs bare at night. His foot is almost healed,
the bones screwed together, re-strung with tendons

from a dead teenager, who was at least alone in his
Camaro as it came apart on 85 near Charlotte.

That could've been you, my father says, how you
used to drive, then remembers I'm less his son already,

the process cumulative, accelerating. He mentions
another trick if piss won't work, will buy a garbage

bag of hair from a salon and cast it through the field.
And I'm thinking of all the haircuts I never wanted,

trimmed always far above brow line, and imagine him
scattering what fell from every forced summer buzz –

hours worth of shears droning at my scalp, a barber
shuffling the checkered floor, one a pervert with his

hand beneath the nylon cape – and how much different
it might have been for me, the other way around,

had I been born a girl but was really a boy, hair blond
and grown long by summer and the heat too much,

begging a five dollar cut, and to run nearly bald across
the ballpark as long as other boys would let me. Deer

still range below the field each night, become their own
loose ring of seasons in this drought-made decade,

and even Lake Jocassee's baring mud except dead center
where no children swim, its turbines slowed and power

dimmed. My father will still limp from living room
to kitchen, kitchen to front door, stooping the gravel

drive to welcome me beyond his own startle and
amazement, whomever steps from my familiar car,

softer now, with rounded face, hips wide as
my mother's, who cannot look at me so very long.

Jordan Rice

Birthright

When my mother speaks to me again there's been six months
of silence between us since I said she lost her son when I was

young and understood myself to be misshapen, but knew saying
so would cause her god so swiftly to descend in vengeful wrath

upon me, neither ashes nor the memory I'd lived and been her
child could remain. I'm asking so I can find you if I have to

call hospitals or morgues. And I'm not breaking down this time,
but am refusing all apologies and closeness and whatever else

she cannot offer first. And only because I took away the body
that she gave me, can I answer her in this voice with my name

to tell her my own father didn't recognize me last month
in a bookstore, but smiled kindly, and kept on looking for his son.

Alfonzo Moret

The Confessant

2009 Collage, image, inks, & acrylic paint. 17 x 20

This painting has to do with my departure from the Catholic Church. I confessed to my priest that my Catholic stepfather was sexually abusing me. The priest told me I should remember to "honor your father and mother." "Even when they are hurting you?" I asked. This image depicts my departure from this faith and my search to find an African God who would accept me.

Daniel Chan

Isaac

After Isaac got down the mountain, he asked his father
      what he would have done
if the voice didn't intervene,
if a ram didn't show up   as substitute.
Would he, still, have run
      the dagger down his soft glowing throat?
Abraham replied *I'd have done what the Lord*
      had told me to do.

      In the old days, two men
          found sleeping together
died to stone. In the old days, a town
      where men slept together
was burnt, like witches.
And I promised: no more "gay" poems,
but here I am   at this confession box wringing out
      my love for men. Here's my father still waiting
          for the punch line,
the plot twist, waiting for some God
      to loosen his choke on the trigger.
In the old days, a ram, or a cow, or some poor beast
      was laid on the altar. Then it was cleaned,
then it was drained of blood.   I'm not sure of the order.
But I know I was bathing, and I know I was losing
      red, and I know
          I was saving everyone the trouble.
And here comes the part where the butch nurses come running.
And here comes the part where I bounce on the stretcher.

And here's the part where the hospital lights
                        are strangely green and I fall
            in and out of sleep.
In the old days, man placed his hand on an animal,
            and that was that. The animal became sacrifice.

When my father wheels me out, taxi door booms,
            hospital shrinks away. I feel my hands
being bound, blindfold drawn over eyes,   the silver of knife
flashes
            as the cab thrums uphill.

H. Melt

Sororicide

the night my sister
taught me to read

my parents
were out
the house

she grabbed the thick red
webster's dictionary with
bible thin pages
I always tore

michelle
demanded I recite
the meaning of sororicide
the killing of one's own
sister

I stayed awake
for years fearing
she'd butcher me
in my sleep

I'm no longer
across the hall
the other side
of a thin wall

she no longer
has a sister
to kill.

Jerrold Yam

Communion

Standing and facing the table with the book and cross,
I don't know if my limbs could afford it,
or what I should be asking, mired
in a swarm of sinners. Lifting
an arm, its fist and fingers, and a
wafer at the end of it, quiet
as a baby's sallow iris, this could be
the one action I cannot get right,
lifting and praying, getting-prayed-for,
the one irreconcilable motion of the
human body. But at the month's
rebirth I would still linger
in its corridor of second chances,
trusting prayer to lead me back into myself,
my own fabled kingdom. Can no one
be without a place? Only disciples
survive on his memory, only their
tongues would reel from the welding of flesh and
blood in a mouth, the wafer crumpled
for swallowing; I am eating
as they ate, and drank, and met again.

Jerrold Yam

Psalm

That night, I didn't know what came over me.
A scene of two characters kissing
brought me to my knees, my elbows
folded on my thighs the way soldiers
prepared for execution, the
human body scrunched and twisted as if
back in its maker's womb. I asked
for wisdom, as Solomon did, anything
to help me understand my making,
if I was thoughtfully constructed
according to plan, if every move of mine
inked its immortality in the loving
pages of your hands. I didn't have a choice.
I didn't have a choice. For years
doubts rode my back like distant travellers
and I tried not to think of them, to be
infinitely echoed in mirrors of self-pity. But
not that night. Tears and mucus
like two rivers married across the barren
plateau of my face, pungent
drops scattered on the wood I knelt on, I finally
knew how the biggest and brightest boast of humanity
would never be mine. Here I am,
pure and unkissed, completely surrendered to
the fearfully and wonderfully made.

Jerrold Yam

Police

I will watch for breathing, hints
of unclasped arms, fallen
apart like hinges. Across floral pyjamas
her pulse uncoils, head perched away
from sun. Then my fingers are
scouring the pages—I know where she keeps them—
under relics of pictures, bills, recycled bags
is her loot of Marie Claire magazines. Sometimes I wait
to hear the drumming of fruits split
and cleaved dry, or an iron's hum
lacing my father's shirt like secrets. In my room
the shirtless males are memorised, unedited
counsel of a better parent, before Grandma returns
I place them back, not an errant fibre
breaking the calm, no cause to make it
any harder to love me.

Jerrold Yam

Invincible

It could be kindness; lakes of neon made
every gesture its own ablution. And
the older guys relented, from practice,
to pandering after a boy's touch,
liquid purity. He loved how they
lifted his face as water to their faces, his
17-year-old cloak of velvet running amok in their hands
like a river over stone. When the pills
slid down his throat, his body gearing
for that saintly climax, everyone in the room
cheered. It didn't matter where
or when he woke up, there would always be
cash by the sheets, sometimes even breakfast,
sometimes just a pool of warmth eddying
and the hushed oath of a door
falling back in place.

Jerrold Yam

Gift

Even as you change me, patiently
oiling the ridges of my bolts, I know
I am not alone. It could have been
much worse: no home to call my own,
dysfunctional pieces of a family
unhappy with who they are given, mimicking
my inner struggles on the vanguard
of the merciless open. This is when
I thank you for my sister. When I told her,
at a bustling junction
mired in the Orchard Road crowd—
my worries getting the better of me, my eyes
pulling back their timid floodgates, how
I would never get married to have children,
to be the golden boy my parents would
market as the epitome of Christlikeness,
their own pat on the back—she
looped her arm over my back
to say *Don't worry, okay. I'll*
always be here for you.
                    All my life
I had waited to be a victim
of the generosity of love. And I tried
my best—gathering achievements
like a harvest to please my parents
who still imagine work
as sacrifice. All my life I had wanted
family that restrained themselves

from the hypocrisy of judgment. All
I know is this: my sister
is the mercy, the family
I never asked for, but which
has always wished for me to belong.

Alfonzo Moret

Bayou Child

2009 Collage ink, pencil, paint on paper. 17 x 20

This painting's inspiration came from my experience of fleeing the sexual abuse at the hands of my stepfather, and a desire to return to a place of protection. When I was born my mother shouted to the nurse, "What's this? A boy?" She said "there must have been a mistake. This is not my child. He's the wrong color and wrong sex. So you better go back in that maternity ward and find my baby girl."

Danez Smith

Monologue #107
the boy after his mother ask what happened

Mom, remember how fast I was? How my legs blurred the field?

No one could catch me. I have been running for years
yet some days I've barely risen from his sheets.

I see him everywhere. In the faces of the boys I teach,
playing basketball in the park blooming with trash,

in the mirror & the brown backs of my hands. Everywhere
is his bed. I try to sing the black boy an always good thing

but I've seen what we can do
to each other. I wish there was a way not to know this.

Who knew you could be ruined by something
so same as you. It felt like I did it myself.

Am I not now a prison? The cell
I tried so hard to avoid? Look at it.

My body: the temple, the jailhouse.
My body: overcrowded & sunless.

I was such a good black boy. What code-switch
could have saved me from his mouth?

Mom, I remember, always. I know, *we work double
to get half.* I know the streets to avoid after sundown

I know the gift & heavy load of our rusted flesh
the miracle of my twenty-first birthday, the praise song

of my holeless body, but this? This leaving?
I was not prepared to be dead this way.

Danez Smith

Deleted Scene: The Shawshank Redemption

The first time we see Morgan Freeman
he is escaping to the arms of man the color
of cement sky, a heaven behind bars
with his hot, grey mouth & prayerless knees
now living for their own glory, they say:

> *if our God will leave us here
> then we leave his laws with our mothers*

& they fall into the sin that is not sin,
they build a church in the middle
of the cell, a flood in the middle
of themselves, swallow the land
dry by morning, slow to roll call,
spent & joy-struck, having spent the night
calling, calling, calling, calling & answering
in sweat.

librecht baker

to descend upon ourselves

to descend upon yourself
while holding dusk as you dawn
witnessing your brimming rise
necessitates no other approval but your word

waiting for another's approval
is a brittle aluminum fence overtaken
by a weather of perspective binding
you, a plot, inside someone else's fence
casting you from you, a nation amongst nations

and you, a field of wild nettle needs water
to liquidate those knowings that aren't your own
for what you know is an ancestral asset
irrigating your rise, bounding past worn posts
attempting to conceal you undetectable
because your dialect is a polyrhythmic reality

where your presence of flesh swept with winds of wisdom
opens a threshold like a smoking bundle
of cedar, pine, and rosemary
so too are the others of us witnessing you
chanting yes
activating your body's water
and transforming any and all dis-ease

in your transformation of believing in you
you begin to starve that uncertainty crackling
every moment another voice douses you with

i don't approve- of you as you wish to express
your yawning adoration, your love- but
i'm happy if you're happy
for then you gift back that brittleness
that dry well of thought attempting to bend your being
because you, a vessel clearing the ether with your light
invokes the abundance in the others of us
triggers the wealth with which we stroll
flowers our remembrance that we too
are normal and our gardens shall nourish
and because of you
we too can sever from old ways
spit back those rusted fences
and hold reverence for the medicine that is us

Helen Klonaris

Weeds

It was hard not to notice them. They lined the path leading to your front door, giant amaranths you called callaloo, a leaf of which you broke off and handed to me: it's something like wild spinach, you had said, amused by my hesitation: go ahead, taste, it won't poison you. You had names for the weeds that grew up in limestone soil in your front yard, and round the back where grass swayed knee high, and you knew what they were good for too: cerasee toned the blood, blue flower for fevers, and for an upset stomach, shepherd's needle—tiny yellow and white flowers I had seen and ignored all my life; staples of the unkempt corners of yards, of the edges of streets that bordered onto bush, vacant lots, poor soil that seemed not to want to grow anything else of value. You left them to flower and seed. You minded them like wild children, watched them grow with affection, but without intrusion. You let them be.

That night, I smelled limestone soil in the crease of your belly, tasted it where my tongue found the back of your right knee, the hollow of your left armpit; I surrendered then to something impossible, or to an unfamiliar sense of possibility and felt the shadow of callaloo darkening my skin, like a tattoo. I had the sensation I had been a shadow myself, till this moment. I thought, we are impossibly real in a place that is impossibly real. I was afraid to leave your bed, the weighty tangle of your arms and legs round mine, in case I forgot what it felt like to be flesh. I lay awake listening to the syncopated thrumming of our hearts; I watched your eyes flutter side to side under closed lids. I heard myself sigh.

In the days that came after, it was me and you, and you and me. You drawing the curtains in daytime, against the watchful eyes of neighbors. Me drawing you back from the front door to kiss you before leaving the house. In the car I threw a grey sweatshirt across the space between us where our fingers might mingle. Together, we were vigilant in parking lots, in grocery stores and pharmacies, in front of Mrs. Taylor's fruit stand. At a red light I watched as the song between us shimmered and evaporated on the stretch of road ahead. But when night came, in the sanctuary of your bed, that song surged again and we hung on to each other desperate for fingers and shoulder bones, the soft skin between toes and an ankle and heel, the certainty of a broad shin gleaming in the dark, the generous solidity of thighs, and finally, gratefully, that place between them where inside and outside came together.

It must have been the song between us that watered the shepherd's needle, the blue flower, the cerasee, the callaloo, and caused them all to flourish outside in the dirt, and then inside, on the white walls of your house. Behind drawn curtains, at dawn you rose, made us tea from something you'd gathered the day before, and I'd watch you carve giant woodcuts of each plant. Evenings, I helped you brush green vegetable dye you'd made from callaloo onto the wood, and press the panels onto your walls; every few days a new plant appeared. Leaf of life hands, rooster comb, hurricane weed. They seemed to take on a life of their own, turning this way and that, depending on the position of the sun. You had said these were the plants your ancestors used to heal whatever ailed them, and it felt as if we were surrounded, even at night with the lights out.

Selfish, you had called me in the beginning, when I first told you I preferred living alone. I liked my solitude, I had insisted, months ago, inside my homemade church, watching you pick up a rock and rub its smooth grey surface between your long brown fingers. You smelled of sweat and coconut oil, and I had wanted to reach over, take those fingers and pull them to my mouth. I didn't. Instead, I said you could keep the rock, that it was a present to remember me by. You had looked up mischievously, as if you wanted to laugh, but stopped yourself, and I knew my cherished solitude was in danger.

I let you go that night, leaving with the women who had come for the meeting; we were protesting the new hotel development, the potential damage to the coastline. You were fresh back from university, teaching biology to high school seniors; you wanted to be involved. I had stolen glances at you in between questions about government policy and environmental impact reports. And when we were done, I watched you leave, your long purple skirt brushing the ground, your right hand holding the rock I gave you.

Then I dreamed you against my will. You appeared to me the way spirits do, your face as close to me as my breath. I dreamed you a presence behind the story of my dreams. I woke with your breath on mine, I myself breathless, awake, pressing myself into the sheets, the pillow, the rock against your fingers, rubbing.

That Sunday you invited me to your father's church. He was a minister, from a long line of ministers; he was outspoken too, on radio talk shows every week, making sure people knew God wanted them to live well on earth, not just in heaven. You loved him for that.

I met you in the parking lot of New Bethlehem Baptist. The morning sun made the lemon silk of your dress shimmer. Your cheeks flushed as you peered over at my white patent leather shoes, my starched and ironed white slacks, my pink polo shirt, items I had picked up in the men's section of the Island Shoppe. I looked away from you to the front door of the church, at the men in brown and black suits standing on either side, shaking the hands of the people streaming in. I wondered if I had made a mistake, if I should have worn a skirt instead. We hugged awkwardly. I followed you inside. The pews were crowded. Women in white dresses and white hats filled the front section. Behind them families with small children were already singing, were on their feet, already swaying and clapping, the organ and drums and tambourine leading their voices in a celebration I was not familiar with. We squeezed into a row of people towards the back. Women turned to look at us, put their arms around your neck, pulled you to them, kissed your cheeks. They eyed me and said welcome.

I could feel my heart thrumming against my ribs out of

time with the organ and the drums and the tambourine. My left shoulder was prayered against your right. My hands were clammy. My breath came and went in shallow drafts because, on the one hand, I could smell the scent of perfume anointing the arch of your neck and I wanted badly to bring my lips there; and, because, on the other, churches made me nervous.

I remembered the last time I had been to the church I grew up in. We were not singing or swaying or clapping in time with tambourines or drums. We did not sing together in that church, unless it was Easter and we were burying Jesus. And then it was a song of lamentation. A song to bury the dead. That Sunday, I had come to church on my own. I had not spoken to my family in months, which meant I had stopped going to church as well. But it was the Feast Day of the Virgin and I was missing the candles and the frankincense and the thick church walls that reminded me of my grandmother's village in Crete, of the stories she told me of women gathering in caves, in secret, to make offerings of honey, sleeping there overnight to receive visions of Her, the one who could protect women from danger—a hard labor, a mean husband, or no husband at all. How she would say these things in whispers, behind the back of my grandfather; how blue and white stone churches had been built on top of the caves so that women came instead to church, forgetting the honey at home, coming empty handed, the dark caves fading into dreams and myth.

I had decided that morning I would not wear a dress. My mother and I had fought about this the last time I had seen her. I came wearing pants. I came with a jar of honey between my two hands. I stood at the back of the church until it was time for Holy Communion. I had planned to walk to the front of the church, and to place the honey at the foot of the large icon of the Virgin. I was nearly at the front of the altar when I heard the commotion behind me. I saw the priest's eyes glance over my head, the golden spoon in his hand poised between the communion cup and the open mouth of the woman awaiting communion. I felt hands grip either side of me, my arms dragged apart so that the jar of honey fell, shattering against the black and white tile of the church floor. And then I was being walked backwards, out of the church, through the front door, as the congregation, women on the left, men on the right, stared, shook their heads, whispered behind their hands, shame, what a shame.

The music inside New Bethlehem Baptist had lifted all who had not been standing to their feet. A deacon was intoning hallelujahs into the microphone, and I stood there clapping and watching you sing; your eyes were closed, your face glowed, tilted to the ceiling, and I thought you looked so at home in your body, and then too, as though at any moment you could fly up out of yourself, into a place that was not here.

We left without seeing your father. We walked back out into the sunlight. Shading your eyes from the glare, you said, can I see you again? I nodded, yes.

A week later, on the red couch in my apartment, you kissed me. You had never kissed a woman before, but you leaned over while I was talking about wetlands and how they were disappearing and kissed me. At first you tasted like Bermuda cherries. Then, behind the sweet, like Shiraz, red and smoky, so that I gasped and said, Oh, God. You had slipped your hand under my favorite t-shirt, the black one with the spiraling white snake, and pressed it palm open and warm against my naked breast. I had circled your wrist with my hand, wanting to pull you back and pull you to me at the same time.

"You sure?"

"You talk too much."

You were closer to me than my breath. Thick warm fingers of your hair grazed my cheeks, my neck; the current between us hummed like a song.

That had been April, when woman tongue and silk cotton trees flowered and their downy blossoms drifted in the breeze. When the weeds on your living room walls grew thick and wild. By June the weather had changed. You became quiet, introspective, and didn't want to be touched. You said you were hot. You needed space. To breathe. You said it wasn't me, it was the heat. The smallness of the island. There was too much noise, in your head. There was tension in the air. Something that had not been here before. You didn't know what. You said it would pass. You said God was trying to tell you something. You had looked at me with some accusation. A Nina Simone CD I had been playing skipped, got stuck like a record and played the same stuttering note till I went to the stereo and stopped it. By then, you were up and walking to the door. You paused in the room I called my church, said, "Don't you ever think, maybe it's wrong?"

I looked around at the rocks lining windowsills, at gnarled branches I'd hung from the walls, at long streams of osprey and heron and seagull feathers that waved in the breeze from the windows. I looked at the blue and yellow and red scarves draped over a narrow table that held my altar: mounds of shells circling blue and green bottles crusted with colored wax, white candles rising tall from their mouths; a long black and red snake carved from driftwood winding its way between clay figures of Cretan goddesses, their arms stretching to the sky; in the center a statue of a woman's torso carved from lignum vitae wood. And watching over the entire room from behind the altar was the painted face of a woman on a square of canvas, red and black and brown brush strokes strong and broad. I thought of her as the Ancient One, as the Goddess of the Mountain we had forgotten and buried and refused entry into the altars of the churches we knew today, except as the obedient virgin. I thought of her as tiptoeing outside our houses in the streets at dawn, and again just after the sun set, crossing over into our dreams at night. A kind of spirit fugitive, a spirit outlaw. I thought of her every time you and I touched, or made love, had a new idea. Or had questions about old ones.

"No," I said. "I don't."

The weeds on your walls began to wilt and so did we.

On my way to the grocery store next morning I heard two men tell the radio talk show host they were gay. The host said, "You know that's not how God made you, but you sound proud of it anyway..."

The men paused, and one of them cleared his throat, said, "You know, Steve, every morning I drive down Shirley Street. I see this guy in the same spot every time. He's sitting on that mustard colored wall outside Mrs. Mortimer's Tuck Shop. Half his face is a mess of skin and scar tissue, the other half looks like you and me. I heard a couple of guys found out he was gay and decided to punish him by assaulting him with a bucket of lye."

"That's rough."

"Every time you tell us 'that's not how God made you', you're giving guys like them permission to turn us into monsters."

I didn't call you that night. I lit candles in my homemade church. I burned frankincense and watched the smoke rise. I sang old Greek songs my grandmother used to sing when I was a child, the pieces of song I could still remember. I waited for a vision to tell me we weren't wrong.

In the weeks that followed it was you and me and some other thing that wouldn't leave us be. It was you turning your back to me in bed; it was me storming out of bed and slamming the front door shut; me revving my engine on the road outside and all the way home, alone. It was us yelling at each other across the table in your kitchen and a half hour later making up. It was me saying I should have never let a straight girl kiss me. It was you saying why don't you get a job? It was me saying just because it doesn't look like a job, doesn't mean I'm not working; I freelance. I sell words. The space between us had become hard to cross. Outside our four walls a storm was brewing.

I passed Rawson Square as I drove over to your place Saturday evening. Already hundreds had gathered in front of a makeshift stage to protest homosexuality and the abduction, rape, and murder of five boys. Across the square a large white banner stretched: "Save Our Nation". We had heard a group of ministers had spearheaded the rally; your father was one of them. We had heard a small group of gay rights activists had set up camp across from the rally. We stayed home. I fried yellowtail and plantains and mixed boiled potatoes with olive oil, onions, and parsley, but we barely ate. Then the phone rang and you answered, hoarse. I heard you say yes Ma, and no Ma, and I'll talk to you soon. And when you came back to the table you pushed the plate from you.

"My mother is asking questions. Wants to know who my 'new friend' is. What my friend's name is, and who her people are." You tried to laugh it off, but your laughter was tinny, the corners of your mouth strained. And then you began the litany.

"We've been careless. People have seen us together. How else would she know I have a 'new friend'?" You were up and pacing the living room floor. "Remember that day in the video store I introduced you to my cousin and she mistook you for a man? And the time in the car when we missed and held hands at the red light and my mother's sister, Auntie Joan, was in the car next to us? What about the time you were leaving my house and Dante drove up at the exact moment we kissed goodbye – did we have the door open, or was it still closed? I don't remember. Damn it, I don't remember."

I wanted to make you feel safe. I wanted to feel safe too. "But he was still in his car, it was so fast, and the door had to be closed."

It didn't matter what I said; it was as if the voices of the preachers downtown had floated all the way into Shirlea, down Shower of Gold Road, through the white gate, under the door and windows and into the air we were breathing. I felt it too. My throat constricted. You coughed, blew your nose, worried your lower lip.

"Come, sit with me."

You shook your head, no.

You said, "I feel transparent," pulling the curtains to. You said, "I feel as if the walls of this house are made of Perspex," and drew your orange terry cloth robe closer around your shoulders. I offered you a hiding place between my two arms, but you slapped them away: "Everyone can see us."

Then you said: "You should never have come to church wearing men's clothes. What were you thinking?"

"Jesus, Addie."

"It's my father's church. You think you can just go anywhere and be however you want?"

"If you want me to leave, just say so."

"No, no. I don't want you to leave."

We slept burrowed into each other like snails.

The next morning I woke early, made us a breakfast of mango

slices and sour leaf tea. You traced the arch of my left eyebrow with your fingers. I said, don't go to church. Stay here with me. I tugged at your t-shirt. You smiled, uncertain. You let me kiss your chin, the corner of your mouth, your right ear.

We heard a knocking at the front door. You pulled away.

"Adeline, you home?"

"It's my mother. Shit. Stay here." You lurched out of bed, threw on your robe and hurried to let your mother in. I considered climbing out the window, but the windows were obstructed by white wrought iron, crafted to look like birds in flight instead of burglar bars. Your voices sank dully in the humid air as winged shadows played across our tangled bedclothes.

"Your father wants to know what's keeping you from praising the Lord."

"I can praise Him anywhere, Mama; I don't have to come to church to do it."

"I'm worried about you."

"I'm a grown woman."

"That's what I'm worried about. What a grown woman like you doing with that mannish woman who I hear don't even have a job?"

"She's an activist, she freelances. And anyhow, I can have friends."

"What you have in common with her, your friend?"

"Mummy, she's not anyone... You don't have to worry."

I could hear crows rustling in the bougainvillea outside the bedroom window, their big voices trilling a warning under the eaves.

"And what's all this? You don't have enough plants outside, you have to bring them inside too? Looks strange to me. Like some kind of voodoo; get these off your walls, hear me? And I want to see you in church."

"I know. I'll come."

After I heard the door open and shut, you didn't return to the bedroom. I didn't know whether to wait in there or come out. I fingered my keys. I sat on the edge of the bed, making patterns in the carpet with my white high tops. I thought, if it had been my mother visiting, and you half naked in my bed just feet away, would I have said anything different?

I sighed and got up. I crossed the hallway into the living room. You glanced at me, our eyes met, and for seconds I imagined this could be our home, our paintings on the walls, our books on shelves arranged in order of most beloved authors; I imagined my guitar leaning against the white wicker armchair, photographs of my nieces next to the ones of your nephews on the round table by the sliding door that looked out on weeds we knew by name. But we couldn't hold our gaze; I looked away first, and then so did you.

"I'll call," I said.

I did call, but for two weeks your phone rang and rang, unanswered. I imagined the phone ringing inside your house, and you ignoring the ring as you brushed your teeth, poured yourself a glass of water, set it by the bed, turned down the sheets, turned out the lights, lay down frowning at the too warm air and the sliver of persistent yellow light reaching its way in through the crack in the curtains from the street outside. I imagined hearing you suck your teeth as you rolled onto your right side, away from the street, the light, pulling your knees up to your breasts and hugging them, child like. I imagined the weeds on the walls limp, leaves turning brown along their edges, their roots snaking deep into the walls in search of wetness and dirt. And only when the phone rang for the last time, its dull clamour dissipating into the darkness and into the solidity of walls and the fading green of leaf of life hands would you allow yourself the luxury of stretching your legs out to the full length of the bed, the silhouette of wings stuck, suspended in the absence of any breeze.

The following night I gave up calling and drove over to see you instead. I parked my car alongside the white gate out front and slipped through it into your yard. The moon was full, and under its light I could see something was different. At first I did not see what that difference was. Then it occurred to me, on either side of the walkway leading to the front door, the soil had been freshly turned and was bare; the callaloo had been uprooted and cleared, the grass had been weeded and cut, cerassee vines stripped away from the garden fence, blue flower and shepherd's needle disappeared. I felt their absence like a drift of cooler air against my skin, like the coming on of the cold season.

"Addie?" I tapped the door three times. I heard stillness, then movement and clatter, and when the door opened it was your face, softly round, your brown eyes bright as sandstone washed clean after a rainsquall. You didn't speak to me as I followed you inside. Instead you padded towards the kitchen, to stir the pot boiling on the gas stove.

"I've been calling," I said, unsure of whether to stand or to sit.

"I've been busy," you said, stirring.

The walls of your house that had been home to weeds that could cure diabetes and asthma and whooping cough had paled, the plants covered over with a fresh layer of white paint. Shelves once arranged neatly with books, *Bush Medicine of the Bahamas*, *Mangrove Ecology*, *Sisters in the Wilderness*, had been emptied of their contents, which now sat in orderly columns beside photographs, and a small oil portrait of your father benignly looking on.

"What happened? Why are you painting over the walls?"

"I'm renting the house."

I sucked in my breath and concentrated on the only object left on the wall facing the door: a large acrylic painting of an old woman smoking a tobacco pipe. She sat barefoot on the steps of a blue wooden porch, her eyes, like crows', staring back at me, her legs wide, her skirt an orange valley between them. Behind her an open door led into a darkened room. I wanted to disappear into that room, to sit with the old woman, rest my head in her lap.

I exhaled. The old woman was watching me. And I was watching you. You holding onto a wooden spoon and stirring. You staring at your own hand holding the spoon. You breathing in deep, and then turning to face me.

"I'm moving back to Canada," you said, as if that answered everything.

"What's in Canada?" I asked, feeling the drift of my hands and legs away from my body.

I wanted to talk about love, but the word seemed made of airy stuff; the word seemed to come from a long way off, from a foreign place where other people lived. Maybe Canada.

"But this is your home." I waved an arm in the direction of the whitewashed walls, emptied bookshelves, the stripped back-yard – all the wild children uprooted now, and wandering.

You turned from me back to the stove and the pot. Your figure was weary and small under your robe. I watched your shoulders rise, then fall. I watched you bow your head, concentrating on the spoon and the stirring. Under the terry cloth I imagined your breasts were tender and full; I had listened to the ocean moving beneath them, sometimes so swollen it spilled out over your skin, wetting my cheeks, stinging my eyes. My heart was full and aching, my hands loose and empty and aching, and I was about to go to you when you said, "There's nothing for me here."

It had been four months and two weeks and four days and everything I had been yearning to touch and smell and hear was in this room.

"How I feel about you isn't nothing."

"This is not about how you feel."

"We've been having a hard time. But we can't give up, Addie. Not now. Not yet. At least talk to me. At least give me that."

"I should have seen it coming. It was his birthday. I went to please him." You had turned to face me now. Your face flushed. "He brought me up to the front of the church. I didn't understand what was going on. Why everyone was staring at me when it was his day. He stepped down from the pulpit. He stood next to me, had his arm around me. His arm tightened. I didn't know what was coming but I wanted to run. Then he started praying. He said he wasn't going to let the devil take his youngest. He made me say it out loud, in front of everyone. He made me say I wasn't what people were saying."

"I'm so sorry." I reached for your hand but you pushed me from you.

"He had the whole congregation praying for me. He said a spirit of abomination had taken over the country, and he wanted the church to be a congregation of warriors, a congregation of soldiers, to fight for the souls of the ones who were lost. I started to weep. I started to feel lost."

"Baby..." I tried again to hold your hand, to touch you, but you wouldn't let me.

You folded your arms against your breasts. You looked down at the tiled floor, then back at me.

"God wants me to change my life."

"Your father isn't God."

"What do you know about God? You don't even believe in him."

I felt the ghost of weeds pressing in on us. Dogs barked in the street. A child began to cry.

"Look at me," I said.

You shook your head, no, and traced the square tile with a slippered foot.

In the silence I heard a clock ticking, the gurgle of okra soup simmering on the stove.

"You should go."

"There is no place else to go."

Okra soup simmered and its scent crept along the walls, wistful. The old woman eyed me.

"This isn't something that's—" you unfolded and folded your arms, "—possible."

I held my throat; it ached. I was about to turn around; I was about to leave. But something about the okra soup, its scent creeping along the walls, the old woman sucking on her pipe and eyeing me, wouldn't let me go.

I sat down on a bucket of paint. "I was a sophomore in college. It was mid-semester and my parents had come to pay me a visit—at least that is what they said. Apparently they had found letters, mine, to a woman I had been seeing. So, they came up there and took me out of school. Just like that. They took me to a motel, forbid me from seeing her, or contacting any of my friends, made me leave behind all my clothes, my books, every-thing. We were holed up in a motel room outside a New England college town, the two of them in one bed, me in another. In the middle of the night I woke up to a yelling, my father pitching up from a nightmare that he was battling the devil. The next thing

I heard was my mother reading from the Bible. 'Yea though I walk through the valley of the shadow of death I shall fear no evil...' She said, 'Maybe she's possessed.' I eased the pillow over my head and pretended to be asleep. I pressed my face down so hard against my fists, the white sheets, I could hardly breathe. All I could do was pray I wasn't crazy. The next day they drove me through Connecticut suburbs looking for a Greek church. They wanted to find a priest who could perform an exorcism. You know, run the devil out of me. Thankfully, the priest wasn't in."

"They took you out of university?"

"Yes."

"What did you do?"

"Dropped out. Came back here. Became an activist. You know, a troublemaker..."

You smiled, your brown eyes sad. "You are a troublemaker." You turned the stove off. You stirred the pot of soup then put the wooden spoon down. You said, "Take me to your church."

"Right now? It's probably closed."

"Take me anyway."

We drove through town, past the library that had once been a jail, past the harbor where cruise ships floated like small cities, past office buildings and nightclubs and hotels to the other side of town, an in between place that was not west or east, where the Greeks had lived in small blue and white and pink wooden houses with concrete porches before they moved out to neighborhoods where houses had gardens and pools. And as we drove, me in the driver's seat of your car, I thought about the two times I had ever seen brown people enter our church, and how nobody had turned to say welcome.

We parked your car on the street outside. An old man and a dog were sitting on the curb and watched us cross the street to the black gate. The church walls and dome ceiling glowed white and blue. I unlatched the gate and walked up to the double wooden doors, rattled the handle, but the doors wouldn't budge. I knocked and the sound reverberated off the walls, the concrete courtyard, the warm stillness of the air around us.

"No one's home," I whispered to you.

"Show me anyway."

I found a window at the back of the church, nearly at knee level. It was loose. I shook it gently, back and forth, till it shifted, opening just enough to wedge a stick under it and lever it up. I lowered myself into the passage. I turned and looked up at you. I held out my hands.

You didn't miss a beat. You took my hands and you let me lift you through the opening and into a bathroom inside the basement of the Church of the Annunciation. I took out my flashlight from my backpack. We walked through a narrow hallway and up some stairs that led into the altar. Women were not allowed here.

Hanging bowls of oil lit the corners at the front of the altar, their flames darting tongues of light in the darkness. We walked out into the nave. Moonlight filtered through the stained glass windows so that we could see each other's faces. We stood in the center of the church listening. To the flames darting. To the pulsing of the darkness.

You reached for my hand. "It feels so ancient."

"I know."

"I grew up in the church. It was everything. I used to listen to my father practicing his sermons and then I would make up my own. While he was at the front of the church, preaching, I would be at the back preaching inside my head. When the people shouted their amens and halleluiahs, I imagined they were hearing me, saying amen to my words.

"I had a best friend, Angie. One summer she got pregnant. She was only fourteen. They made her leave the church. I asked my father why. He said she was a bad example for other girls. There was a rumor that one of the deacons had been messing with her. But nothing ever came of it. My sermons dried up. My words got lost."

I squeezed your hand. I shone the flashlight up at the altar, there were paintings of the saints – John Chrysostom, Gregory of Nyssa, St. Basil, John the Baptist, St. George spearing the dragon, St. Christopher. All of them old and white and male.

I said, "They're happy when our words get lost. It makes it easier for them to keep talking."

I thought of the white statue of Christopher Columbus a few blocks over on Government House hill, presiding over the town, his sword in the sand something like St. George's spear in the belly of the dragon; I thought of the pink walls of Government House, how you always said pink was a color the English used to lull slaves into obedience.

I said, "Any chance there's a bucket of callaloo paint in the trunk of your car?"

You said, "Yes... what for?"

I said, "Wait for me."

I came back with a bucket and a brush. I peeled the lid open with a key. I stirred the dye with a stick.

"Take off your clothes."

"Here?"

"Yes."

You did. You took off your t-shirt, your bra, your pants. I took off my t-shirt, my bra, my pants. We were standing naked on the black and white square tiles of the church I grew up in. Your breath on my lips. Our eyes liquid. Our fingers hummed. The air electric. Your fingers grazed my breasts. I looked over at the bearded faces of pallid saints. We laughed.

And then I was dipping a brush into the thick green dye, and stroking it on in great swathes across your breasts. Frankincense and callaloo and the muskiness of our bodies filled the air. You pressed yourself against me, our bodies painting each other, then, without speaking, we walked towards an empty white wall. You first, then me, hand in hand, we leaned into the wall, as if it were a third lover. The soft flesh of our breasts, your right cheek and my left, made sucking sounds against the wall; the wall like skin, lips, a forehead. I whispered into the wall, can you feel us? When we stepped away from the wall we had left ourselves there.

You took up the brush and stroked my breasts, then my belly, my pelvis and thighs and shins; you were anointing me... the palms of my hands... there were no nails here, and no crosses... we were not dying... we embraced the wall, again and again, leaving ourselves everywhere... in between wooden pews, in between mourning faces of old men, in between golden wings of angels...

arched around the body of the Virgin... our fingers reaching for each others' fingers, bellies, lips... our bodies intertwining, insistent, against the wall; we did this as if our lives depended on it, as if it were high mass, as if it were a forgotten ceremony erupting out of a fissure in our memories, a waking dream, what was lost is remembered.

As the light of morning began to stream in red and purple and orange through stained glass pictures of Jesus and his cross, Joseph of Arimathea bearing up the cross for him, Mary weeping for her son, nighttime shadows on the walls became callaloo green silhouettes of two women standing, holding hands, embracing, kissing, arms raised high, their legs and breasts and fingers as visible as if they had always been there.

The callaloo had dried on the walls and our skin. We helped each other put on bras, shirts, pants, socks, shoes. I gave you a leg up to the window and when you disappeared, I gripped the ledge and pulled myself out too, out of the altar they said was no place for girls.

Outside, we felt light and airy and large... like our bodies had become giants and our hands could reach over and across town and caress the surface of ocean waves if we wanted to. We chased each other hooting all the way down the hill to the strip of beach at the island's edge; we took off our clothes again; we waded into the water. We used handfuls of sand to scrub each other's breasts and arms. The water turned deep green all around us.

Alfonzo Moret

At Home In The Swamps

2009 Collage Image, Inks, and acrylic paint, on paper. 17x20

This painting reflects back on a time of isolation, when I told my gay friends of color that I had embraced my true faith in an African spiritual tradition. They were fearful that I was someone who practiced Santeria, which was evil, in their eyes.

TC Tolbert

Discourses of Disaster or How does it feel to be alive?

I've been thinking a lot about representation and competition among trans folks. I've been testing out joy as the most vulnerable human experience. Love, I think, is just the insistence of a generous translation. If this is true, I wonder what *family* means. Henri Bergson says, *It is we who are passing when we say time is passing.* CA Conrad says, *Suddenly. And at no speed other than suddenly.* In *The Longest Sun*, an old guy said, *Why do you treat time as your enemy? It isn't yours to lose.* As far as I can tell, object permanence is still a theory. What about the body can we stop? A lesson I want to unlearn: proximity is more dangerous than it looks.

For years I directed a commemorative project that memorialized murdered trans people by building kites. The kites were intended to document not just the deaths but the living. So, I did my research. I read the papers, the blogs, the news reports. *I would like to understand more about compassion*, Maggie Nelson says in *The Art of Cruelty, and I am gambling that one way of doing so is to get to know its enemies, near and far.* What I found was a world that said *unidentified*. Then, later, it called people by the wrong names. Were the kites containers? *Six stab wounds. Severe head injuries. A broken bottle. Stoned. Burned. Raped. Raped. Signs of torture. Shot. Strangled. Shot.* I called the project *Made for Flight.* It seems we still have to die to have a life.

The problem with trans representation in the media is two-fold. The first is what Chimamanda Ngozi Adichie refers to as "the danger of the single story." Victims, hyper-sexed marauding freaks, or comedic relief—trans people can really only be one of these three things. The second is that this story of violence and extreme victimization is true.

Today, November 20, is the 15th Transgender Day of Remembrance. At events all across the world, someone will stand at a microphone, or in a circle, or on a stage and will call out the names of trans people—primarily trans women of color—who have been murdered (at least, those murders that have been documented) in this last year. Today we will read 238 names. Last year we read 265. All told, we've called out 1,374 names since 2008. I actually have to slow myself down in order for this not to become another blip in the information stream. It takes work to not go numb. Kevin Rozario in "The Culture of Calamity: Disaster and the Making of America" says: *Trauma was defined by Freud as "an event the full horror of which is not and cannot be assimilated or experienced fully at the time but only belatedly." It is not "available to consciousness until it imposes itself again, repeatedly, in the nightmares and repetitive actions of the survivor."* Today we will read two hundred and thirty eight names. In the last five years, one thousand three hundred and seventy four trans people have been murdered worldwide.

Adichie says it's simple. *Show a people as one thing, as only one thing, over and over again and that is what they become.* Let me say it plain: for most of my life I've felt broken, not just tarnished. There has long been a darkness, a kind of violence in me that I have feared and of which I am deeply ashamed. This is less about being angry that someone did something awful to me as a kid (although they did) and more about being afraid that I deserved the awful and that awful is what I create. As Adam Phillips points out in an essay on agoraphobia, *James' open space is full of potential predators, but in Freud's open space a person may turn into a predator.* We often turn this external violence against ourselves, and I did the same. I began to see my genderqueer body as separateness, personified. A sign of everything that was unlovable about me. That, in fact, no sane person would rightly want to be with someone so shattered and so stained.

As a protection from this fear and this pain, I've spent plenty of time contemplating suicide—sometimes more actively than others, but the gist is this: I held onto it as an option. There was something about knowing I could leave this body if I needed to that made me feel safe. On some level, no doubt, transitioning was a way of killing my most vulnerable, marked self and an attempt to make peace with men – a group of people I've long considered the enemy. Indeed, as I had sex with my ex and we played out violent fantasies unsurpassed in my previous experiences and embodiment (suddenly I really was "the man") I was frozen by a multifaceted terror that, at its heart, was simple. I was afraid of becoming the thing I longed to be, needed to be, hated to be, and asked to be so named.

But that's only part of the story. Maybe the real shame we all grapple with is that any narrative coherence is a myth.

Here's another version. I recently went to a movie with a friend. We biked there but walked home afterward, pushing our bikes so we could have more time (space) in which to talk. My friend is moving soon. Or rather, she's already left but she's back now and now she's leaving again. I wanted to kiss her but I didn't. It means something different now for me to walk slowly with a woman in the dark.

What the papers never say is *boring. Jealous sometimes and competitive*. Or *pretty*. They never say, *made a mean chicken soup with some fat back. Loved the sound of a vacuum*. Never say, *annoyed her friends when she sang off-key in the backseat. Smiled when she danced dirty but kept her eyes closed. Had a tattoo from the Bible on her back*. I'm not talking about mirrors, exactly, when I'm talking about how to broaden trans representation. What the papers never say is *living*. What we never get to see, what I'm looking for, what I'm trying to show you, is *changing*. Something to see in, yes, but something also to help us see further. What I'm trying to find, to feel, is *alive*. A simultaneity to see with and see through.

Alex Simões

sobre morrer

Para Nilo Alcântara, in memoriam

quem deu um tiro em tua nuca
e te amarrou os pés, te pôs
num saco sob a terra, pois,
deve ter mais fundida a cuca

quanto fundida a minha está
quem põe os rótulos, quem diz
como se deve ser feliz
o que será e não será

vem do poder que alguns arrotam
a língua o sexo a cor a classe
saber de quem olhar a face
temer objetos que nos cortam

lições que as ruas pedagógicas
nos dão em doses alopáticas
da morte surge a matemática
dispondo os corpos noutra lógica

horizontal te vejo eterno
retorno ao pó (quem dele escapa?),
a vida a gente assim solapa
eliminando os rostos ternos

vai-se o caixão, ficam meus dedos
atravancados nesta terra
quem ama mata morre berra
aprende ama o próprio medo

neste vazio em que ora habitas
uma canção, teu manifesto,
loas à tez, à mais bonita,
deuses de Ébano te empresto

that Black is beautiful, my Lord
embora em línguas de outras gentes,
façamos nossos os acordes
que dizem mais sobre viventes

Alex Simões

on dying

translated from Portuguese by
Tiffany Higgins

for Nilo Alcântara, in memoriam

whoever fired a shot into your nape
and dragged your feet, placed
you in a sack under the earth, then,
must have a messed up head

as messed up as my being
whoever classifies, sorts, who says
how one ought to be happy
or what will be or will not be

comes with the power that some boast
of tongue of sex of color of class
knowledge of whomever looks at surfaces
and fears those objects will cut us

lessons that streets of pedagogy
give us in doses that are allopathic
of the death that arises from mathematics
disposing of bodies with another logic

horizontal I see you eternal
returned to dust (who escapes?)
life, us, undermined thus
eliminating any tender faces

the great box is off, my fingers remain
blocking this soil
whoever loves kills dies bellows
learns loves his own fear

in this emptiness which you now inhabit
a song, your manifesto,
you praise complexion, most pretty
I loan you gods of ebony

that Black is beautiful, my Lord
out in the tongues of other peoples
let us make our own accords
to speak more of those now living

Alex Simões

eu canto pras paredes

o preconceito é uma parede enorme
contra a qual desde sempre me empurraram
mas se tentaram e não me executaram
é que aprendi bem cedo que não dorme

o apontado: preto bicha pobre
no paredão cresceu e ficou forte
ainda com a dor que o véu da morte
bem do seu lado alguns amigos cobre

e é por eles que não me vitimo
nem quero mais derrubar a parede
apenas canto para além de um íntimo

desejo reforçar rizoma e rede
cheia de nós, que não estou só, sou vivo.
picho a parede: meu verso afirmativo.

Alex Simões

i sing through walls

translated from Portuguese by
Tiffany Higgins

prejudice is a wall, enormous,
against which forever they have pushed
me. but if they tried and didn't execute me,
it's because I learned early that who's in the lineup

must not sleep: poor black queer
on the big wall grew and got strong
still with pain that the veil of death
of friends at his side collects

and thanks to them I don't victimize
me, nor wish any longer to break the wall
I merely sing beyond to my intimate

I desire to weave rhizome and web all
full of us, so I'm not alone but alive.
I spray paint the wall: this verse affirmative.

Alex Simões

Soneto À Ladeira Da Montanha

Photo by
Sônia Maria Chaves Nepomuceno

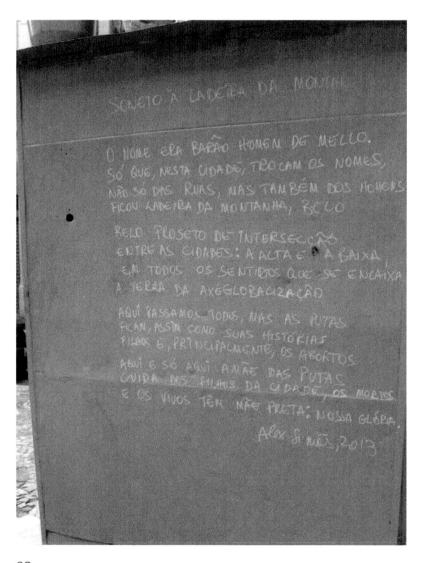

Alex Simões

Sonnet to the Ladeira of the Mountain

translated from Portuguese by
Tiffany Higgins

In Salvador, Bahia, ladeiras are steep alleys connecting high city from low city. Axé, a concept of African origin, denotes cosmic spirit.

The name of the street was the Baron Mello.
Only that, in this city, they exchanged names
Not only of streets, but of men.
It remained the Ladeira of the Montanha, bela:

Beautiful project of the intersection
Between cities: the high and the low,
In all the senses that enclose
Our land of AxéGlobalization.

Here all pass through, but the whores
Remain, along with their stories,
Sons and, especially, the aborted.

Here and only here: Our Mother of the Whores.
Cares for the sons of the city, dead
And living who share a black mother: our glory.

Fabian Romero

Drugs and Capitalism:
How Sobriety is Part of My Resistance

> *"The trouble is that once you see it, you can't unsee it. And once you've seen it, keeping quiet, saying nothing, becomes as political an act as speaking out. There's no innocence. Either way, you're accountable."*
>
> -Arundhati Roy

I cannot write about my reasons for sobriety without talking about all that makes me who I am. This includes experiences of racism, cissexism, ableism, nationalism, poverty, and anti-indigenous sentiment. This includes the ways my awkwardness, anxiety, and depression have shaped me. I cannot stress enough that I believe that addiction is a form of genocide supported by institutional power. It's no coincidence that poor, black, brown, and immigrant communities are at the center of drug and alcohol exploitation. For these reasons sobriety is part of my resistance to the institutional oppression and exploitation of my people. There has been a legacy of exploitation from the moment that colonizers set foot on our land to the present. I recognize that sobriety is only one part of my resistance to oppression and that I am not superior to people who use substances. I support and respect addicts and alcoholics who are not sober or practice harm reduction because they are still my people.

Recovery

I don't know what life was before pulque and the spirituality that came with it became marketing for tourism in the landscape of

Michoacan. I only know at night the spirits came out, both in bottles and in bodies. Cactus spoke of the history we hold in our melanin, too painful to understand. There are borrachos in my family, drunkards forgotten in the cities, lost in prisons and underground.

When my family left Michoacan to search for a way out of poverty I thought we had left alcoholism behind. I have only seen my mother drink alcohol once in my life; my father a handful of times. They are both scarred by the abuse and excuses of addicts and alcoholics in their families. Although they don't speak of it or acknowledge it I know that the disconnection from our indigenous roots also holds part of our story. I have in my body Purepecha blood so powerful that I feel earth speak stories. I hear how the Europeans introduced alcohol to Indigenous people in the North; how pulque and all spiritual practices that utilized mind altering substances were vilified. That before the slaughters came the friars arrived with assimilation trainings and shame for our ways of life. Given that mind altering substances were considered sacred and used for rituals before colonization, I wonder if addiction came with the settlers. I wonder if it was another disease on top of smallpox that we contracted from the Europeans and Spanish. Regardless, this disease has had a hold on my family for centuries. The land my family acquired during the Mexican Revolution has mostly been lost or sold to pay off debt from addiction.

I was the last of my friends to start using drugs; a late bloomer at 16, I fell into it fast. In short I became sober because my depression, anxiety, and subsequent awkwardness got to be too much and I relied on drugs and alcohol as my only means of relief. My belligerency overwhelmed the revolving door of friends; the substances no longer worked, and I found myself alone and miserable. To me, this is connected to genocide and institutional power. Although I was unaware of it, I was battling deep insecurities rooted in racism and all the forms of oppression I navigate daily. Science these days has caught up with what our bodies have carried for centuries, that oppression causes depression and anxiety and to medicate I was turning to what was readily available in the neighborhoods I grew up in. The suburb of my youth was overrun with condemned houses from meth labs. It was there that I was introduced to drugs and alcohol as a teen by my then boyfriend, who survived by selling drugs. We were in the prison pipeline and many people from my youth got caught or died too young. There are years in my youth and early twenties that are marked by obituary clippings and funerals. People like me in coffins. I remember the phone calls still, how sometimes I knew the news before picking up. I don't know why I have made it when so many people have not and will not. I believe it is partly because I am practiced in politeness and my light skin privilege benefits me that I have not ended up prison. I believe it is my ancestors watching over me that I am not dead like I thought I would be by now.

Although many promises were made to myself and others about changing my self destructive patterns, I was twenty-four when I began a recovery program. This program worked for me for a few years. I could meet and talk to people who were also struggling with addiction. It was what I needed then, a structure to fall back on and people who would listen, but as time went on I realized I needed more.

It wasn't until I returned to Mexico for my grandmother's funeral that I felt the weight of my history fall onto me. Drug cartels were visible on the three hour drive to my home town; on road sides I could see armed men guarding trucks and merchandise. I felt my mother's hand grip me as she had in other times in my life; these are the men we avoid. These are the men who cause the trauma that generations of women carry or die from. Drug cartels are linked to gender violence, poverty, and exploitation of women, especially Indigenous women and children. Indigenous communities in Mexico, as in the United States, are sites of state sanctioned violence. As my car arrived at my birthplace in Michoacan, a pueblo two hours away was beginning to arm itself in order to protect its people from such forces. I have followed the news and heard mis tias' fears rising from reports of missing people and increased military visibility. My mother in turn warns us about visiting; she puts emphasis on me. I would stand out among my people, my gender expression too visible and easily detectable as someone who comes from the States.

My sister stays in touch with a distant aunt from Mexico City who shares links on Facebook regarding the gruesome violence directed at children. This on top of the stream of deportations puts a stress so heavy on my family that I wonder if it is possible for our bodies to carry grief of 100,000 to 1,000,000 people. There are various numbers out there about the casualties related to the drug cartels, but since they are partnered with the United States I will add in the number of people who died trying to emigrate to escape the poverty, violence, and injustices caused by powerful drug lords and their militias, including the Mexican police and United States government. I choose to stay sober to resist the violence directed at Indigenous people, trans and cis women, and children in Mexico caused by drug cartels.

Politics of Borders and Drug Wars

I still feel the deep impact of borders. I am one of the lucky ones, a child with parents who did not get swallowed by the desert, a cousin of many family members still alive in different cities around the United States; lucky because I keep track of the numbers of people detained or deported. I have known from childhood that borders are meant to control people and simultaneously protect wealth. Drugs are part of that wealth, and poor people are exploited to maintain it on both sides of the border.

This is not just a Mexican problem. It is global and is supported by Western powers. Through an investigation on the Bush administration it was revealed that the U.S. government made a deal with the Sinaloa Drug Cartel. It is one of the biggest and most gruesome organizations centered in Mexico City. Some of the agreements from these deals allow the drug cartel to smuggle drugs into the United States and grants the dealers impunity from the murders, violations, and crimes they commit in exchange for information. While these deals were being made the drugs were shipped to major cities in the United States with the approval of government officials.

I know stories of close and distant family members who chose to risk their lives for a shot at a different life. Drug cartels have grown in places where people are desperate for a shot out of poverty, and unfortunately there are a lot of people willing to do this work if it means feeding themselves and their dependents. Much as the United States preys on brown, black, and poor people to fight its wars; the cartels preys on children, women, poor people and Indigenous communities.

Institutions and Ableism

I have experience in institutions that profit off of addiction and drug wars, including prisons and rehabilitation centers. In rehab I gained the trust of the doctors who boasted about the amount of money they made. I learned that like prisons, rehab runs on recidivism because they were never created with the intention of healing addicts. They were born out of asylums and created as a place for the affluent to cover up an affliction attributed to the poor and uncivilized. Historically some of the most undesired people have been disabled people. Alcoholism and addiction is a disability, as in not functioning normally and undesirable. For these reasons it is important to talk about disability justice and ableism when talking about addiction. Prisons were once the holders of all undesirable people, and from prisons came asylums to hold people with disabilities, and from there came rehabilitation centers. They are all connected.

My first two years of sobriety were spent working with incarcerated youth. I saw first hand how the drug wars here are pushed to increase longer drug sentences for brown and black youth. Black youth especially. Many of these youth were immigrants. Many of these youth grew up in rural and suburban towns throughout Washington and like me experienced poverty and exploitation. Many of these youth had parents in prison for drug charges. It was then that I began developing this political understanding of sobriety and how prisons and immigration reform are all connected.

So while the drug cartels struck deals with the DEA and ICE, detention centers exceeded their monthly quotas with undocumented immigrants, and new private prisons were being built throughout the US. I know now that it is all connected. The people who profit from addiction are connected to the DEA and ICE. Meanwhile the propaganda push for a drug war reads like a call to incarcerate brown and black people and immigrants at all costs. Prisons are disproportionately populated by marginalized people such as the disabled, trans women of color, youth, immigrants, and people of color. Prisons also profit from this and would not be successful without capitalism.

Capitalism

In an interview about his book *River of Smoke*, Amitav Ghosh is asked about how his research on how the opium wars of 19th century China compare to today's drug wars, especially those in Mexico. He replies by saying that there are a lot of parallels including the Western world's "huge trade deficit in relation to China." His continues by stating that the United States maintains its "economic supremacy" by "ratcheting up the rhetoric about 'Free Trade' 'Liberalization' etc." and have chosen to forget "that this rhetoric was first deployed in defence of opium." He takes it further by stating that "the first major testing ground [of capitalism] was opium." Free trade, the root of capitalism, is traced back to opium in China and now over 160 years later is still feeding off of drug wars and the consequences of drug trade.

So again, I cannot write about my reasons for sobriety without talking about all that makes me who I am—all the experiences of racism, ableism, cissexism, nationalism, poverty, and anti-indigenous sentiment that I have lived through. I cannot stress enough that I believe that addiction is a form of genocide and that it is connected to the prison industrial complex, US imperialism, and capitalism.

When I was nine I found out one of my most loving uncles had passed away. Cirrhosis of the liver. Although I have lost many family members in drug and alcohol related deaths, his continues to be one of the hardest lessons in life. I was warned early on that our blood does not do well with drugs and alcohol. Some say the spiritual disconnection from early colonization made our blood susceptible to addiction. I chose not to listen, and I am certain that at my bottom, before making the decision to become sober, I felt the grief of capitalism and colonization. It was then that I felt my body take on the grief of 1,000,000 people. I decided then that my sobriety was not just to save my own life but to honor those whose grief I carry. My sobriety is resistance.

Ahimsa Timoteo Bodhrán

Vergüenza

He didn't realize the shame of being Native was the same
as the shame in being queer. The shame of wanting to touch
something, someone, his hands reaching towards trees but
looking around before touching, or touching so brief it
might be brusk, might bruise the branches, tear a leaf, rip
acorn from what was once tender grasp. Soon he wondered
the ways in which, during the years he has closeted, was his
touch sometimes quick, veering to be discovered, and still
now, out with it all, was he wondering, wondering with
that, wondering in what further ways he refrained, wanted
to, refrained again, from touching the limbs of men, their
warm trunks, their strong bodies, and did he turn from them
the way he turned from trees, unfortunate, into the night?

Ahimsa Timoteo Bodhrán

rough

we sniff salts to move us back into consciousness.
give me the recipe for ammonium carbonate.
too rough, you said, in my hands,
even in bed too eager, left you sore where you didn't want to be.
this baby born without lotion.
yours was a high class mixing.
mine, ghettos y barrios, people who'd never flown in a plane,
only knew this land. yours, a diplomat's diaspora.
tus padres: modelos. *your six languages?*
lose count, stumble with my few.
i trade you mango-wet kisses by the projects.
roaches scatter.
you see the world laid out wide before you.
i see stones in the path, am checked for weapons at the gate.
you float on through, emptied oysters at your lips,
pearls and abalone around your neck.
my soon-to-be-revoked passport.
you are always arriving, and i always waiting for departure.
comment on my way of eating,
my inarticulate manner of speech.
you shift red to my blue at this station, Doppler effect.
hurtle life. i am surprised our trains do not collide.

Ahimsa Timoteo Bodhrán

geographies

My ex is on the corner buying drugs. I take
the first flight, then the second. tire
marks are still on the wall. I enter
the building we lived in together. rabbits
of decayed animal carcasses jump
across the floor. two-tone paint
jobs. On the roof
of the apartment building we now
share, I stare
north, look out over El Barrio, up
2nd Avenue at the Bronx, homeland.
You tell me
it is Harlem still. I insist the island shorter
on this end.
Grow cold, go below,
colder
than this weather.
Use the pages of a subway map
to keep warm.

Ahimsa Timoteo Bodhrán

Repatriation

National Museum of the American Indian, NYC

In the museum of our people, I take you by the hand,
through the exhibits. It means something to kiss you here.
By the exhibit on Native skateboarding and (land)surfing,
I take your tongue into my mouth, and you, mine.
Interesting
to think: We are protected. Our art and bodies, for once,
protected. People need to go through security to get to us.
Perhaps this is where we are most safe: behind glass,
security guards. People can't say shit, or there'll be
consequences.
You're gonna say something to two queer Native boyz in a
Native museum, really?
Who knew this is where our kiss-ins should be? But less
protest, and more affirmation.
We come home.
At places the general public can't
enter with weapons. Past the electric wands and electric
gates, where you have to pay admission to see us. Perhaps
they will bring offering. Centuries in waiting.
Grand Entry.
Perhaps this is where queer powwows
can occur. Where urban Indianz can go. We can make out.
Have our 49er songs. Imagine 1491.
We seal the deal with a kiss.
Amidst other works of art. I
take you here before I make love to you. There is a pattern,
processional. A protocol for mating.

I will take you here; then we will eat. Then we will eat, again. You so good against my tongue. You, the one treasure I stole from the museum.
Repatriated.

Celeste Chan

Still from the short film "Bloodlines"

2011: An experimental ode to immigrants detained on Angel Island during the Chinese Exclusion Act.

micha cárdenas

Excerpts from "Redshift and Portalmetal"

We have found
ways to shift the light in the air around us,
so at times we can be completely invisible
going through border checkpoints,
and sometimes in our own communities,
at other times we shift the light to see each other
beaming with color
redshift
plumshift
blueshift
two femmes hunting non-transfer lipstain
building knowledge
so we can colorshift into our full spectral brilliance
and hold our individuality, in relationship,
each moving at different velocities,
each radiating their own hue,
moving in shared orbits.

Space is cold, dark.
We travel in tunnels underground that spit us out into tiled
rooms.
We learn technologies of warmth,
technologies of sustenance,
and give them to each other as precious gifts.
Walking above ground,
I see a transporter go past with a photo of a planet on its side,

shaping my imagination of this space I inhabit.
Waiting in the underground tunnels,
I see photos on screens of my home planet's dying ecosystem.
We have no home to return to,
intergalactic diaspora.
My father also took flight,
from the violence neocolonialism brought to his homeland,
in a silver and orange arc in the dark sky,
yet the planet he landed on was as
hot, humid and fecund as his own.
The icy surface of this place is bright, reflective,
I watch it through the windows,
disappearing under snow, again and again,
as we hold each other tight to stay warm.
We need to build homes where we go,
to carry them with us, and in us.

I'm building a home, here on this planet of ice.
Always felt like an orphan,
even on my own planet,
like there was no one to protect me but myself.
Shuttled around without ever feeling like I belonged anywhere,
between races, cultures, genders and sexes.
I built a femme science,
a science of
learning to build homes,
learning to keep myself safe,
learning to let others in.
But I'm not doing it alone,
from out of the void,
I'm doing it with so much help from
my love, who has lived here always.
I know this is my place now,
on other planets, the inhabitants stare at me,
like an alien from a foreign galaxy,
my body not fitting their idea of human girl,

but here, I feel at home, safe.
Safe is a foreign feeling,
I'm just learning to relax into,
yet I can't stop working
to undo the laws, the architecture, that allows me to be here,
even while I'm benefitting from them.
The walls and agents and maps that make both
the settlers and the first peoples of this place
into aliens and natives, oscillating and refracting.
We'll build a new world
give this land back to its original inhabitants,
and ask them if we can stay,
this is the only ethical option.

micha cárdenas

We Are The Intersections
From "The Transborder Immigrant Tool" series

[32' 53 6.4608 // -117 14 20.4282]

Working on the Transborder Immigrant Tool was a given for me.
After years of creating electronic disturbance online,
Ricardo and Brett came to me with a plan
to create border disturbance, at the intersection of
recycled electronics and networked gps satellites
To use cell phones to direct people attempting to
survive the desert of the Mexico/US border to water.

[25.684486, -80.441216]

My father fled the violence of the drug war in colombia,
and ended up in miami, kendall drive and 152nd avenue.
My birth was a result of the neo-colonial policies
sending weapons and neoliberalism to colombia,
and a result of the endless hunger of the US for illegal drugs,
the same drug war causing massive non-violent
uprisings across Mexico.

[32.71215, -117.142478]

Six years ago,
3,000 miles away from miami's
anti-castro anti-gay anti-communism
away from my parents' catholicism, both irish and colombian.
I finally found a queer community and an activist life that
supported me in being the trans girl I've wanted to be for so long,
after leaving another activist community that
couldn't handle my transition and wanted me to go to
the men's group.
Last year,
thanks to the femme wisdom of my lovers and friends,
thanks to the femme science we are developing,
thanks to spironolactone,
prometrium,
estradiol,
I started passing as female,
passing enough to get harassed on the street.

[32' 50 26.4402 // -117 15 31.6542]

Walking around as a femme in most places,
feels like walking around being hunted.
I am conscious everyday that I live in a country, the US,
that silences victims of sexual violence and often provides
more safety for rapists than for their survivors,
every night as we walk home from wherever we can find parking,
often in dark alleys or poorly lit streets,
since we can't afford housing that includes parking.
Fearing for our physical safety,
constantly avoiding the men who stare at us, leering,

is perhaps a nanoscale molecule of the feeling of being
hunted by the Border Patrol that migrant people feel
when they cross borders.
Hungry eyes like hollow circles of night vision goggles.
The year that I finally felt that people saw me as a woman,
was also the year I joined so many women I've been close to
who were survivors of sexual violence of some kind.
In January,
I learned I was a survivor of sexual violence I could not
remember,
committed by a family member, incest.
First came the numbness,
then came the paralyzing fear of telling anyone,
the fear of being wrapped up and
written off in a narrative of pathology.
I was reminded of the words of
Professor K Wayne Yang to his students:
You may not choose to be in this war, but you were born into it.
Perhaps, again like how people born in the global south feel,
in countries like Colombia and Mexico,
terrorized by war and poverty,
do they feel that they were born into it,
that through no fault of their own they are survivors of violence,
like me? Violence of colonial steel walls, corrugated and mesh,
akin to the force of sexual and gender violence,
We are constantly navigating the violence of borders of all kinds,
skittering across earth
pinging satellites
that never correctly know
our exact locations,
for they never know how many kinds of thirst we feel.

[34.088705, -118.281894]

Now this fierce mixed race transgender incest survivor
queer femme pornoterrorista
is even more unraveled, bare,
stronger,
even more pissed, behind her eyeliner, in her too red lipstick,
leather V heels and her black miniskirt dress,
even more ready to burn and
create and dream new worlds into existence,
where the logic of western reason isn't used to uphold some
false image of nations and laws that
mask the absolute violence faced by so many who step
outside of the borders, or who are born outside of them,
or who choose to cross them.
and I am here to fight and fuck and give birth
to border disturbances,
to queer and mayan technologies that can reveal
national borders for the fictions they are,
to technologies of survival and femme disturbance.
I am the intersection, of too many coordinate systems to name.
We are the intersections, and
we exceed the borders placed upon us.

Janine Mogannam

sacred city

burning post-conservative emissions. cooling our simmer.
endless summer.

bodies breathe. ribbons of green cut through concrete. i sit on
cliffs with the light, look south.

silhouettes crossing borders. lost limbs. every breath heavy.
air smells false fresh.

remains of a real city. its namesake would cry. morning of light:

my window to forgotten saints. only my television smiles.
neighbors drown me in hostility.

the sun burns cool. (she has endured others.) the eucalyptus
hate me.

i abscess concrete. exhale anxiety. sanity is lost to the horizon.
self-conscious, concealing. breathe heavy. drown in thick air.

is the ocean death or freedom? salt city beribboned in yellow.
inhale.

heat suffocates lungs. i dream burned freeways & scarred bodies.
the city smells of loss.

i drown. can't reach shore. body sacred no longer. the ocean a
tangle. this sacred city:

searching and never finding.

Janine Mogannam

the view from bethlehem

i.

the wall cut through her backyard.

it took from her everything she knew.

the road to her sister's home, gone.

her sister, gone. the soldiers watched from tall towers

as though *they* were the trapped princesses.

she couldn't breathe. couldn't see the sky. only this stretch

of concrete.

her skin turned pale as the afternoon sun no longer shone

on her face. she wilted.

she faded.

ii.

the wall curved itself into her consciousness,

panel by concrete panel.

she woke up thinking about it each morning,

thinking about the fairy tales

where young women are trapped

in tall towers, waiting for rescue.

but in her story, the dragons

are the ones in the towers, watching,

fiery breath poised,

and there is no magic, no rescue.

no way over the wall.

iii.

we drank local beer on this side of the wall

breathed fragrant *arghileh* clouds into our lungs

while just on the other side

the soil told tales of blessed ones

smashing bottles into skulls

& beating red blood

from broken sons.

Janine Mogannam

meditations in an emergency zone
after frank o'hara

our bodies are made of war.

sometimes the kinetics are so intense
we can do nothing but wait.

oh, mother. it is here
in your arms we are loved.

do not allow the ~~entrails~~ hemlines to drag on the ground.
please keep all *decolletage* covered.

now we remember the tombs.
grandmother procured the key.
east jerusalem, we are free.

we sat in the gutters, here.
little baby bones. skull candy.
not only two thousand years ago:
today, now.

tonight the stars are outshone by ~~bombs~~ fireworks.
we drink anise liquor until everything is glitter.
dance like tribesmen under the moon. behold, jesus.

the burning is just a few miles away but ramallah
is a city of stones. it is oz. i cannot breathe.

i spit on the ground and the world turns.

Janine Mogannam

found on her soil

palm trees
olive trees
pine trees
dahlias roses birds
of paradise *majnoona* (plant
& woman) date
trees walnuts apricots
mint sumac thyme
pomegranates pesticide
plaster: crumbled
concrete
glass
wood
stones
so many stones
gunmetal
landmines
bombs: American
in origin
shrapnel
bullet shells
bones
teeth
bones
teeth
fire (air)
fire (blood)
fire
*

Indira Allegra

Protect You

2011 Jersey cotton, linen, batting, thread. 7.25" x 7.5"

Protect You suggests the record of Native future and legacy be reclaimed by indigenous hands, to be crafted with ink, stitches, and woven cloths.

Indira Allegra

One Land One People

2011 Denim, jersey cotton, paper, batting, thread. 12" x 14"

One Land One People is a banner under which urban Indians from North America and South America can exist in allyship with one another—where the Eagle and Condor meet.

Ahmunet Jessica Jordon

Submission

I keep my feet on the ground
for fear of flying too close to the sun.
The rays turn skin into tar. Black ashes.
On the ship we were planted bodies against bodies.
Toes dragging, scraping at the dirt.
Trees kept our secrets in the late night air.
Stars formed formations of freedom.
Don't dare go near the light. It will burn your vision.
Turn your dreams into ruins.
We buried hope in the ocean's waves.
Engulfing sand scriptures.
Our skeletons made timelines on the sea floor.
Bones turned into cities.
Sunlight turned flesh into ashes.
We never knew the new world could be so hot.

Rajiv Mohabir

Bound Coolie

In the Guiana cane fields, it was commonplace
for a man to turn to another man,
to loosen his baba and to stare as the clouds
race across the sky, especially in the rainy months,
I expect—those kajri months of *my lover*
lives in which country—the truth is
that there were few women to caress
bound bodies—the truth is queerness
was a tool for survival, a trade wind to sail a kite
then cut its cotton string. I imagine
the cane fields, the foliage teeth burned
away, blackened, dotted white in strewn
dhotis and pagris of men, inside
men's mouths and fingers—
like on the platform where one night
in Fort Hamilton I waited
on a Queens bound F train when I knelt
before the Trini dread and he sky gazed
dreaming of Chaguanas and frigate birds
only to see the crash and the spark of
the metal rails inside Brooklyn's belly.

Rajiv Mohabir

Haunting

Every body is a haunted ruin: the hinges
of bone and bone, and the binds

grafting limbs into movement wears
into broken chandeliers and cathedral

stones. What echoes of prayers
are scrimshawed along the length

of femur and ulna that beg for *just this once*?
I only write you in loose friction.

Along the ventricles the lights are out
and you feel your way through

the sanctum into finality. At the basest stone
of your house you strike your foot

as you come in from the rain. Your every step
away from our bed etches its likeness

in the thin fictions that slide between us.
In this building of shattered whispers

I say your words in the dark to taste you.

Alfonzo Moret

The Winged Believer

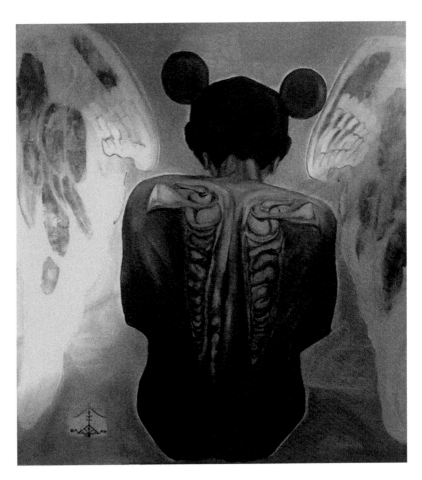

2011 Acrylic Painting, 48 X 48

This painting depicts my ex lover who died of AIDS in 1999. I refused to believe he was dead. Every night I would call his house hoping he would pick up the phone. One night after my calling ritual, I returned to the kitchen and suddenly the room was filled with a bright golden light. I felt arms surround me and pull me in close. Then a voice behind said, "What's in the pot, baby?" He would often tip toe in then grab me around the waist and whisper these words. I was so shocked and pleased to see him again. I could smell the Three Roses Hair Oil he used. I tried desperately to turn and see him, but he wouldn't let me. He said, "you wouldn't recognize me now. You remember me in one body, but I'm not in that body anymore." So I just stood there in tears, holding on to him for as long as he held on to me. Later he said, "Don't mourn for me, I'm in a good place now, no pain, no judgment, you must release me now." Then he faded away.

aaron ambrose

out building

from the inside
barn walls split
the night stars into strips of light

this is where I went
just a little one
in diapers
in the night

I fled my room
navigated hallways and stairs
the back door
down the long dark road
into the stables across the way
with the horses
taking me in

I slept

those animals were careful

stood like sentinels above my little body in the straw

as a toddler I knew in my bones
my brand new bones
what housed love and what housed pain

taking

to the open air
moving toward safety
is instinctively

human

buildings speak

they are steeped and breathing us

my grandparents' home was sealed tight
the stiff still distance between us all
breached only by midnight grabs for flesh

that staid house smelled like men

the meticulously clean room corners
held shadow loss
echoed hungry
poisoned women
recycling the air

I was a child that practiced leaving
practiced night air cracks
in the walls
practiced letting go

bone flight is wired into me
nothing feels
as good as a door shutting behind me
fresh air
on my face
on the dirt path

out
to where earth holds court

I'm wired for night stars

no poison
no clean
hungry
corners.

aaron ambrose

homage to making do

from the roof of our house
we can see the mountains
down to the foothills
down to the endless tightly knit rows of rooftops
boxes full of heart beats
wrapped in traffic
engraved with arroyos
severed by highways

finding ourselves
in the ebb and flow of fumes
that move thru doors
windows and bodies
the always present yet silent
radiation into the skin

our blocks watch santa fe
downtown eastside foothill money
from a distance
the wealth decides
our neighborhood is the labor
not the art

here is where our queer hearts
beat
home
this low down
stucco frame house
with asbestos floors

and hollow doors

we give it spoonfuls
of beauty
battle the dim rooms with sunlit lust
offer up luminescent schemes
give anger a place to burn

and like the house
our own wiring is, you know,
a little sketchy
we are worn out gorgeous
built on decades of questionable decisions
and beyond our control collisions

it gets crowded in here

hearts beating in every available space

we make elbow room with our laughter
make sense of it all over dinner
raise garden beds of children
growing like morning glorious weeds

we mind our neighbors

smile say hello in the street
watch all the children
climb over block walls
to connect

queer crip love pushes
back doors open for air
welfare lungs exhale
the dirty carpet truth
on those turn the heat up darkest days

there's love in ebbing the poison

there's love in witnessing
the illness and the ache
painting patience
teal and gold
the sun says
it could be worse
maybe soon
says hey, today
we've got it pretty good

just sit a minute

crack that window

look

the sky's blue.

Jennie Kermode

Interstitial

I have not been beyond these walls for five months. If you disregard visits to the hospital, it's two years. If you consider the walls within my skin, it's twenty.

The first signs of the disease appeared when I was fourteen years old, just around the time I came out as bisexual. Although that's when doctors first noticed my hormonal differences—the four years of hell before they came up with a temporary fix—it would be a further fourteen years before I found out I'm intersex. It was then, in the toilets at school amid the homophobic graffiti and the stink of piss, that I found a small, hard lump on my head. Six years later there was another, on my chin. I went to the doctor. *Is it cancer?*

No, he said, but he couldn't tell me what it was.

That year my partner developed leukaemia. I would spend the next ten years as a carer, more indoors than out. I was lucky. This first stage of my imprisonment coincided with the internet beginning to expand. I found occasional pieces of work there. I spent time with friends. Within my 2x2 metre study, the universe was spreading out.

It was when my partner was going through a bone marrow transplant—the most dangerous part of the process—that my own disease was finally formally diagnosed. By then there were more little lumps, now pushing up through my kneecaps, causing the joints to swell up with fluid so I could barely walk. It would be years before I could persuade anybody to help me with this. My doctors were more worried about the muscle wasting, the general skin damage, the danger to my heart and lungs and kidneys. In due course there would be a stroke, an eight day coma. On awakening, one of the first things I checked was that my genitals were intact. We hear stories, people like me, of doctors tinkering whilst we're unconscious, taking it upon themselves to help us to be normal. As if normal were that simple.

Now the walls within my body are a cage; just under the skin, a second skeleton, armour of calcium carbonate. The rest of the damage has taken its toll and it's hard to recognise this body as mine. Too late, a new drug, suppressing the advent of new symptoms. Too late, anyway, for going back.

We want to fit this treatment around your lifestyle, my consultant used to say. *We want to make sure you can still do the things that matter to you, like your work.*

Yes, I can still work. Yes, I do. But what about dancing late into the night beside beachfires bulwarked against the fury of the North Sea; what about picking up strangers in fetish clubs and waking up in graveyards in the chill of an Edinburgh dawn; what about staggering home in bloodied ballgowns on a Sunday afternoon through urban wastelands where the seagulls lay claim to the remnants of civilisation? *No, I don't need to work on my knees,* I would tell him; but there are others things I want to do on my knees. There is more to life.

It took me a while to realise that I couldn't go back. That even if the cage walls were broken, even if new stem cell muscle tech gave me back my strength, I couldn't return to that world. It's not about age; the world is always full of opportunity. It's not about the loss of friends who swiftly forget what they don't see, or what they prefer not to look at. It's about what the layers of walls have become. The cocoon.

What does the caterpillar understand of the moth, or the moth of the caterpillar? Is all the former's learning lost during the process of transformation? Does it retain any sense of self? It is broken down at a molecular level, much as my flesh has been broken down. The same pieces of this biochemical jigsaw, reassembled, produce a very different picture.

Within these walls, my world has split. I interact with the macro—with politicians, governments, broadcasting companies, tilting the direction of the world. I interact with the micro—with the mice who wander through this room in search of food or sex, the insects that come and go each season, even the tropisms of the plants. Life is fractal; what we perceive, what we influence, and how much it matters, depends only on the scale at which we choose to pay attention to it. For me, the middle layers are missing. It's rare that I speak in person to more than two people in the course of a day. I hear others passing by, I drink their conversations, but the walls shut them out.

I used to fight what felt like hopeless battles for equality I never thought we'd get. Now that my body can no longer serve, no longer be there to press up against walls of riot shields or take a beating to speak its sincerity, I fight with words to change laws, and things are getting better, but I don't know if I'll ever sample the rewards. I am tending to a world that I am no longer a part of.

Within these walls, I am reformed. It is not simply that I have become comfortable with my sex, nor that that in turn has helped me come to terms with my non-binary gender—it's that in this world, neither sex nor gender has any real relevance. They subside into the chemical soup. I wonder if what eventually emerges will be sexually of interest to anyone. It may very well be partly robotic. Gone are any concerns about passing as normal. These days I have to drag up to pass as human.

I'm not sure I mind.

The walls that had seemed to cut off life have instead revealed a realm of possibility within, an opportunity to live and to understand life in ways wholly divorced from the familiar mandates of social survival. *One morning, when Gregor Samsa woke from troubled dreams, he found himself transformed in his bed into a horrible vermin,* and nobody noticed.

What prisons do we habitually construct for ourselves out of the perceived approbation of other people?

When you're out and about, walking through the city at night, look up at all those walls, at all those lights, and ask yourself how many of those within are part of your world, how many are strangers to it. Within every major city there are hundreds of people like me. We observe you passing by. We drink your conversations. Your poorly guarded thoughts pass into us, blending with the strange elements of our new flesh.

Visiting ancient ruins, it's easy to equate the masonry with the civilisation that built it. But it has never been the walls that matter, only the spaces in between.

July Westhale

A Wild Applause

I.

I am haunted by the pink edges of Oakland, the horizon stretched
out like tenderized meat. It's not a city that people live in,
it's a city gorging itself on goddamns, and it knows this. The
knowledge of this is heavy, Latinate, botanical. In all places, fig trees
bow over the sidewalk and let their wide skirt flaps dangle,
the Queen Anne's lace and wild valerian covered in shattered glass,
light fracturing like a disco. The day goes up like curtains going up—
a wild applause and starts again, the operetta, a steady wail
of shopping carts, a supersonic crowd, wild geese, a lake of bodies,
and the creatures in backyard lagoons. I say thank you, to the sky,
open like a hot mouth in a humid city. Thank you to the
pomegranate trees, the full churches, the graceful gait of people
leaving and entering paradise. Thank you to paradise, how
complicated and enthusiastic.

II.

Soothe me, Huey Newton, soothe me. Your face on 55th and Telegraph,
your daughters in the well-oiled spokes of the AC Transit buses.
My neighbors are buying fruit from a truck down the street, their hands
like pale weasels dipping between the citrus in the geometry
of produce. They come in and out of the steady houses, awnings
fawning over them and coronating their steps. Cars wait for them.
They live in a beautiful country ruled by no one. My neighbors
are eating their avocados from Chile, the California to the South,
my mother's face in the pit, shining like a spit-slicked womb. This town
is beauty, all warehouses and fierce days, sun pulling the sky

into a toothy grin, all windows open like musician's busking
or egrets in flight. I walk cautiously, afraid of borders.

III.

How come, despite all this, you never mention the families before?
The brown grandad's to the white Michigan-natives, who flocked
in like pelicans in heat, or like graceless sea urchins with their non-
native spindles, weaving all the straw into gold? Everyone knows
San Francisco is a city built to emulate Greece, built up in the minds
of union contractors whose mothers saw the ships arrive. The city
is white. It pushes all of the shadows and ink and nuance to
Oakland. And when it is done, it raises its sail, and pushes off.

July Westhale

Un Aplauso Salvaje

I.

Estoy persuigida por las afueras de Oakland, el horizonte estirado
como carne ablandados. No es una ciudad donde vive gente,
es una cuidad de conchasumadres, y lo sabe. El sabiduría
de eso vale pesado, latinado, botánicamente. En todos lugares,
arboles de fruta madura bailan por el piso y dejan sus faldas
abiertas, las tulipanes y valerio salvaje cubiertos en vidrio roto,
la luz fracturando como una discoteca. El dia va arriba
como una cortina corriendo arriba—un aplauso salvaje,
y empieza de nuevo, la operatta, un grito constante
de carros de supermercados, un multitud supersónica,
gansos salvajes, un lago de cuerpos, y las bestias en lagos
de patios traseros. Digo, gracias al cielo, abierto como una boca
con calor, en una cuidad húmido. Gracias a los arboles de granadas,
las iglesias llenas, la manera de gracia de caminar, la gente
saliendo y entrando paraiso. Gracias al paraíso, que complicado y
emociante.

II.

Suavizame, Huey Newton, suavizame. Su cara en 55th y Telegraph,
sus hijas en las ruedas acietadas de los buses de AC Transito. Mis
vecinos compran fruta de truco unas cuadras de allí, sus manos
como animales pálidos entre el geometría de los limones. Vienen
y salen de casas constantes, puertas roncando con sus salidos y
coranando sus pies. Autos esperan por ellos. Vivan en un país
magníficos, fallo por nadie. Mis vecinos coman paltas de Chile,
California del Sur, la cara de mi madre brillante en la semilla. La

cuidad es belleza, todos fábrica y dias fuertes,
sol seguiendo cielo en sonrisa de dientes. Todas las ventanas
abiertos como aves volando. Yo camino con atención, con miedo de
las fronteras.

III.

¿Por qué, con sabiduría de todo, nadie me avisaba sobre la gente
anterior? ¿Las familias morenas, los abuelitos mesclados en vez
de los nativos de Michigan blancos, que llegaron como pelicanos
en calor? Todos saben que San Francisco es una cuidad grecia,
construido en las mentes de organizados uniónes, quienes los
madres miraban llegando los barcos grandes. La cuidad es blanca.
Lo saca todo el sombro, y los matices de tinta, a Oakland. Y cuando
termina, se va en multitud.

lee boudakian

Imperialist New

to be new.

to be waking up anew.

as though for the first time.

ze, waking up from a difficult sleep.

a heavy   empty

sleep.

as though the place ze was coming from was no place

was a void

was devoid of space, or ground, or earth.

it was a place to float

and suddenly: green.

from side to side: horizon-wide. up and down. from inside the

ground. from toe to

head.   green,   and green from brown.

brown.

the colour of the sun kissing mixed up skin, kissing through the pale coat ze wears through winter months. the privilege of a pale coat. the way it divides mother from child. privileging the patriarch. the preferred father. drunken white. ever absent. always longed for. always preferable to perceptions of angry, cold, shut-down

"you ungrateful little bitch!" snapped momma. and slammed the bedroom door, leaving little ze to stare blankly into her palms.

remembering the sun, as the rain pours down, washing brown down the drain... ze wants to be a diver. To jump into the pool of glistening...
ze remembers the sunny breeze
sitting on the grass as blue shorts came to meet hir.

"wow, you get so dark in the summer," white in blue with eyebrows raised and pink lips turned into cheek corners, "like a person of colour, dark."
    "i am a person of colour."
    "oh, really?" he pauses. "are Armenians really POC?"

"we're also Lebanese."

"really?!"

his surprise made hir nose tickle. more like itch—the
way ze itches for summer sun as the winter days have come. The
night that only breaks for a few hours of grey.

nights of rain drops on window sills,

windows next to beds,

beds where sleeping bodies rest.

sleeping bodies hibernating.

to be new.

to be waking up anew.

as though for the first time.

ze, waking up from a difficult sleep

To be waking up as the rains have come,

To be waking up bleached-

in a bed of sheets.

> *"We are NOT middle eastern," she snapped.*
>
> *"Well what are we then, mom?" ze asked.*
>
> *"Are we West Asian?"*
>
> *"We are Armenian!"*
>
> *"And Lebanese."*
>
> *"That's where I was born and raised."*
>
> *"And Syrian."*
>
> *"That's where dede's side of the family is from."*
>
> *"Why is our skin brown?"*

"We aren't brown."

"Well, what are we then, mom?"

ze remembers momma's stories:

> *"Black, black, Bodak!" kids called after them.*
>
> *"Stop it!" momma cried at bullies who beat her brother*
> *blue.*

ze remembers momma in the mirror, painting black eyes green
and brown lips pink. she painted them   with thick sticky paint.

　　　　　　　　　　　　　　painting eyes and lips shut.

but (silent) stories get passed down—from mama to child.
tearing open seals,   ze rips skin off flesh.   exposing the red.

> *"I don't believe I live on Native land," the*
> *student proclaimed, "And I don't like the implication*
> *that I'm a visitor here. I was born here."*
>
> *The student batted lashes at blonde*
> *administrators who turned to the rest of us and*
> *said: "These are sensitive issues, ladies."*

　　　　ze—sometimes she, sometimes he, but no part
lady—thinking back through empty sleep,

as though empty were real—

as though floating were possible without strings

As though empty was not built on

visible backs, held in place by

visible hands and shoulders,

as though visible is not a colour.

to be new. to be new. to be waking up anew

as though for the first time.

ze/we waking from a difficult sleep.

a heavy.

empty.

sleep.

as though the place ze was coming from was no place. was a
void.

except that place was some place.

that place is here

Heidi Andrea Restrepo Rhodes

The Other Side

I.

To see behind walls, delved vessels, diluting pretense,
majestic interludes dissolving grim partitions, feet on ruins
bulwarked in the name of sanctuary, or preemptions,

we map ourselves by the light of hesitancies and moon,
piece by piece, layer by layer
against the immurements of this age, the suffocations
of mandates, the endorsements of our corseting, we never
feel the fullness of we, of our fine-tuned strange,
these edicts clothing us, asphyxiating the tender shine
of our scarlet radiance, secrets, the pouring forth of marvel, and

I run my fingers over cold broken pieces, brick, rubble,
like tablets speaking four thousand commandments
of loving in a time of fear, like tombstones declaring
the beauty of,
                    like the grinding of rocks between our molars,
we suck the bones of our caging,
                    tongues seeking marrow, hungry for,
        hungry for, hungry for,   and

I run my fingers over my cheeks, walls holding in teeth,
holding in words,
                    every letter of every name, the old names of our want,
                    the quiet names and raucous names

of every staggering loneliness,   the pittance
        of company behind an abundance of divisions, doors,

with the flame of your teeth you scale me, climbing over me
searching for what was on my other side: the side of dreams,
        the side of unleashed compositions, balladry, song,
        the side signed 'x,' illiterate or uncharted, peculiar,

I lean my ear up to it all, and trace
        the soft worn years holding it all in beneath
                the audibility of screams

        and that place where the stones have worn
        from your years of knocking

II.

This wall of bones, chapel of memory ossified,
stacked femur columns, the oblivion of gold
                in the crevices of teeth,

skeletal arches, metacarpal daisies, and mud,
ghosts whispering appellations, forgotten,
last spoken in the wind of
long ago midnights, or yesterday
the delicacy of skin, muscle, tendons,
frailty of bodies rent under the edges of occupation,
tired resistance, future rage coded
        into the chromosomes of our birthing,

tonight I weep for the children who were
        my cousins, grandmothers,
five hundred years old, stacked into the pillars of churches
to fortify mud and straw sheltering priests and kings
from the torrent of jungle rain
            and the violent mourning wax palm canopies,

tonight I stand how many thousands of miles away,
across borders,
distant geographies,
       the other side of our wayward memory, the other side

of hells you lived,
the other side of bone-walls, ghosts breathing onomastic tales,
wailing grief, the bitterness of broken ribs,

I kiss your lips, and remember their names,
and there too, your teeth room the chronicling of violence,
of your grandmothers, of genocides,
and the cracked sidewalks, skulls,
split lips of today's antagonisms,
and all the contempt of righteous boots, fists

there, in a kiss, we scale the wall of bones,
we scale our own teeth, facing
our dismemberments through mnemonic histories, there
in the crevices of concrete, from ash, from
                        the wreckage of centuries,

small yellow flowers, bougainvilleas blanketing stone, arias of
freedom,

we scale the ache to bloom home.

Heidi Andrea Restrepo Rhodes

El Otro Lado

translated to Spanish by
Vivian Lopez

I.

Para ver detrás de paredes, vasos ahondado,
diluyendo pretensión,
interludios majestuosos disolviendo grave particiones,
píes en ruinas
en el nombre de asilo, o interrupciones,

nos mapeamos por la luz de vacilaciones y luna,
pieza por pieza, capa por capa
contra los emparejamientos de esta edad, las sofocaciones
de mandatos, los endosos de nuestra encorsetamiento, nunca
sentimos nuestra plenitud, de nuestro afinado extraño,
estos edictos que nos visten, asfixiando el brillo, tierno
de nuestro resplandor escarlata, secretos, la efusión de maravilla,

y paso mis dedos por piezas frías y rotas, ladrillos, escombro
como tabletas que hablan cuatro mil mandamientos
de amor en tiempos de miedo, como lapidas que declaran
la belleza de,   como la molienda de rocas
                                        entre nuestros molares,
nos chupamos los huesos de nuestros enjaulando,
lenguas que buscan ósea, con hambre de,
        hambre de, hambre de,   y
paso mis dedos por mis mejillas, paredes que sostienen

dientes, que sostienen palabras,
cada letra de cada nombre, los nombres viejos de nuestro deseo,
los nombres tranquilos y nombres estridentes
de cada impresionante soledad,   la pequeña cantidad
de compañía detrás de la gran cantidad de divisiones, puertas,

con la llama de tus dientes me escalas,
trepando sobre mí buscando
lo que estaba a mi otro lado:
          el lado de sueños,
          el lado de composiciones desatadas,
                    de composición de baladas, canción,
          de el lado firmado "x," analfabetos
                              o desconocidos, peculiar,

inclino mi oído a la altura de todo, y trazo
los años suaves y gastados sosteniéndolo todo debajo
                              de gritos audible

          y ese lugar donde las piedras han gastado
          por tus años de golpeteo

II.

Esta pared de huesos, capilla de memoria osificada,
columnas de fémur apiladas, el olvido
de oro en las grietas de dientes,

arcos esqueléticos, margaritas metacarpianos, y fango,

fantasmas susurrando títulos, olvidados,

hablando por ultima vez en el viento
de las medianoches de antes o de ayer,
la delicadeza de piel, los músculos, los tendones,
la fragilidad de cuerpos se rompen bajo los bordes de ocupación,
resistencia cansada, furia del futuro codificada
en cromosomas de nuestro nacimiento,
esta noche lloro para los niños
        que eran mis primos, para mis abuelas
quinientos años de edad, apiladas en los pilares de iglesias
para fortificar fango y paja, dándole asilo a curas
y a reyes de la lluvia torrencial de la selva
        y de los lamentos violentos de las palmas de cera,

esta noche me paro cuántas miles de millas lejos,
a través de fronteras,
geografías lejanas,
        al otro lado de nuestra memoria rebelde,   al otro lado

de los infiernos que viviste,
al otro lado de paredes de huesos, fantasmas respirando cuentos
onomásticos, llantos dolorosos, la amargura de costillas rotas,

beso tus labios y recuerdo todos los nombres,
y allí también, tus dientes guardan las crónicas de violencia
de tus abuelas, de genocidios, de aceras y cráneos agrietados,
labios rajados de los antagonismos de hoy,
con todo el desprecio de botas justas, puños,

allí, en un beso, escalamos la pared de huesos, escalamos
nuestros dientes propios,
que enfrenta nuestro desmembramientos
de historias mnemotécnicos, allí
en las grietas de concreto, de ceniza, en las ruinas de siglos,

pequeñas flores amarillas, buganvilla cubriendo piedra,
con arias de libertad,

alli escalamos el dolor para florecer de nuevo.

Trish Salah

Offer the desert, the tower
(with apologies to Adonis' *Mirror to Beirut*)

From the café she watched the stranger's arrival.
The minaret wept: He bought it and troped it
with a chimney.
Suppose the era spoke so bluntly:
You do not belong.
Would you answer bluntly:
I do not belong.
Try to understand, this *now*
of a shadow, lost in skull tangles.
You see from your feet, the wall spoken of,
is a fence the distance shrinks.
The window cedes daylight threads,
to strip my lungs, to stitch the evening.
All this recurs in silence:
Recourse of a stone under my head.
Now a rose, now live coal,
overfull with contradiction.
Like the moon, always wear
your person in a stone helmet
to fight your own shadows.
The door closes on pale handfuls—
Light fails, words fail to convey our gratitude.
Killing has changed the city's shape.
This rock catches bone. This smoke, peoples' breathing.
They— we— no longer meet. Promises
dig the space enclosed until soil remains
our only meeting point.
He shuts the door, not to trap his joy
...but to free her grief.

The newscast:
About a woman in love, being killed
A boy being kidnapped, a policeman growing into a wall.
When it comes, it will be old.
When they find people in sacks. They found people
without names, parts— Without parts of themselves,
without selves, limbs, looser than ever Sappho,
or any lyric poet, wanted.
(Should we not say what she wrote? The objection to his writing,
such things?)
When it comes, it will be old.
He was not a murderer, he was a boy.
We say, he once was sad.
Her voice, vibrating—there is no homeland—
and now she's fluting in air.
Tears for an eclipse, friends' departed
tired of the breathing of people.
Taking sides with the stones:
Trees bow to say goodbye
Flowers open glow lower leaves to say goodbye
Roads like pauses, between the breathing and the words say
                                        goodbye
A body dressed in hope, falls in the wilderness to say goodbye
The papers that love ink, the alphabet, the poem speaking
Say goodbye.
Fugitive threads, reading, the crying flowers
after thought of reason,
after thought of prayer.
You do not die because you are created or because you have a
                                        body
You die because you are the face of the future.

Trish Salah

قدّم البرج للصّحراء

translated to Arabic by
Nayrouz Abu Hatoum

(مع الاعتذار من أدونيس وقصيدته "مرآةٌ لبيروت")

راقبتُ وصولَ الغريب من المقهى.
أجهشت المنارة بالبكاء: فقد اشتراها وأجازَ إستعارتها
بمدخنة.

تخيّلي لو تكلّمَ الدهرُ بخشونة:
أنتِ لا تنتمين.
هل كنت ستجيبينه بفظاظة:
أنا لا أَتنمي.
حاولي فهم أنّ ظلّ هذهِ " الآن"،
قد فُقد في حَبائكِ جُمجُمة.

من خلال قدميكَ سترى الجدار المذكور،
سوراً هو البعد يتقلّصْ.
أقحمَ الشباكُ ضوءَ النهارِ خيوطَه،
ليُجرّدَ رنّتيّ، ليخيط المساء.

كل هذا يعودُ في الصمتِ:
لجوءَ حجرٍ تحتَ رأسي.

قد أصبح الآن زهرةٌ، فحمٌ حيّ،
مشبَعٌ بالأضداد.

كالقمر، إرتدي شخصَكِ
في خوذةٍ من حجر
لتحارب ظلّك.

يَغلِقُ البابُ على قبضة يد شاحبة-
يفشلُ الضوء، تفشلُ الكلمات في الإبلاغ عن شُكرنا.
غيَّرَ القتلُ جسدَ المدينة.
هذه الصخرة، تقبضُ على العظام. وهذا الدّخانُ، تنَفُسَ الناس.

هم- نحن- لم نعد لنلتقي. وعودٌ
تحفرُ المكانَ لتحصرهُ فتبقى التربة
نقطة لقائنا الوحيدة.

يُغلق البابَ، لا ليحبسَ نشوَتهُ
...بل ليحرّرَ حُزنَها.

نشرةُ الأخبار:
إمرأة عاشقة، تُقتَلُ
طفلٌ يُخطَف، وشرطيٌّ أضحى جداراً.

حين تأتي، ستغدو كبيرةً في السن.

عندما يجدون الناس في أكياس. سيجدونَهُم
من غير أسماء، أعضاء، من غير أجزاء من أنفُسِهُم،
من غير أنفسٍ، أطرافٍ، أرخى، من أي رخاوة كانت سافو،
أو أيّ شاعرٍ غنائيّ، يرغب بها.

(ألا نقول أنها كتبتْ؟ إعتراضُها لكتاباتِهِ، هل من شيء كهذا؟)

حين تأتي، ستغدو كبيرةً في السن.
لمْ يكن بقاتلٍ، كان صبياً.
نقول، ذاتَ مرّة كان تعيساً.
صوتها، يرْتَجُّ- لا وُجودَ للوطن-
وترفرفُ الآن في الهواء.
دموعٌ نخبَ الكسوف، رحيلُ صديقة
قد ضاقت عليها أنفاس البشر.

في تحالُفها معَ الحجارة:
تنْحني الأشجار لتنْطق الوداع
ببريقٍ من أوراقها السُفلى تُعلنُ الورودُ الوداع
طرقٌ كالبرهة الزمنية، بين التنفس والكلمات تقول وداعها
جسدٌ يرتدي الأمل، يَهوي الى البريّة ليقول وداعاً
ذاك الورق عاشق الحبر، الأبجدية، الشعر
يقولُ وداعاً.

خيوطٌ شاردة، تقرأ، بكاءَ الوردْ
خاطرةٌ من الرشد،
خاطرةٌ من الصلاةِ.

لن تَمُثْ لأنكَ خُلقتَ أو لأنكِ تملُكين جسداً

تموتُ لأنكَ وجهة المستقبل.

Trish Salah

Poem for Abousfian Abdelrazik

Between states, I can only imagine, your being
suspended, in a fiction held, an interminable nowhere.
Suspended, do you imagine return to a some where being?
What's home, having travelled this far held some where no
place, near real. Longing, an out from an imaginary state?
Living is the embassy of a country that denies you home.
Unimaginable life suspended, in the siege of a terror, law
(the failure of law), a terror you're allotted like skin to wear.
Do you feel your self a person, do you hold your self still
waiting for air, for an outside, some place where you know
desire's flight, and the price of a ticket? Terror is years
cut out from home, your name effaced—we hope, no longer.

Trish Salah

إهداء لأبو سفيان عبد الرازق

translated to Arabic by

Nayrouz Abu Hatoum

بين دولٍ، أكاد أتخيّل، وجودك
مُعلَّق، مَحْصورٌ في قبضةِ روايةٍ، في اللامكان الأزلي.

مُعلَّقًا، أتتخيّل عودةً لمكان ما وُجوديّ؟
ما الوطن، وقد سافرتَ هذا البُعدَ مُحتَجِزٌ في مكان ليس

بمكان، يقاربُ الواقع. أشواقُ، من خارج وحي دولةٍ متخيّلة؟
هي حياتُنا سفارةٌ لدولةٍ تحرمنا الوطن.

حياةٌ - نعجز عن تصوّرها - معلّقة، في حصارِ الإرهاب، قانونٌ
(إخفاقُ القانون)، إرهابٌ مفصّلٌ لكَ كالجلدِ ترتديه.

أتشعر بأنّ شخصَكَ إنسانٌ، هل تَكبُدُ نفسَك ساكِناً
تتوق للهواء، لخارجٍ، لمكانٍ تعرفُ فيه

رغبةُ الطيران، وسِعرَ تذكرةِ السَفر؟ الإرهاب هو سنواتٌ
بُتِرتَ فيها من الوطن، وحُذفَ فيها اسمُكَ - نتمنى، ألّا يُحذف أبداً.
لكل ما تشتهي.

Minal Hajratwala

Labyrinth

I listened to gulls wobble like doves,
thrash of ocean or highway.

They broke my spirit as man breaks horse, bit by bit. I felt the bit
behind my teeth—press of tongue, cold metal wet with spit.

Orange juice burned the morning off my tongue, acid searing
its pink depression, cells coated with nightmare's residue.

The dust of my silence thickened into this mudwall between us.

I ate the *prasad*, matzoh & gefilte, rock candy, gold raisins, wine,
    wafer. Raising my eyes, I saw clouds, stains, an impenetrable
    blue.

I heard a man read Sappho on the radio—all wrong. They want
    to use us, even our words.

Throats cracked as we sang *holy, holi, wholly*.

Only the prostitutes in the temples know God. They have sucked
    & fucked him, run their fingers down his spine & up his
    cavities, heard him moan & beg for more. "God," they like to
    say, "is one ugly motherfucker." It is one of the few pleasures,
    one of the few truths left.

I twisted my pubic hair, braided myself closed. Strange pimples
    grew all over my skin.

Under their weight I did not try to buck.

In bed anxious alone I reached for the steadying wall, nubbed
with layers of paint, smeared insect palimpsests.

I was the wide heartbeat, infinity between inhale & exhale. Solar
hydrogen burst in my cells like fireworks, independence, the
pursuit of happiness in milk mugs filled with tea & glittering
spices whose English names I did not deign to learn.

I bowed to the hem of my sari so they could not see the tattered
stitches, tears rolling upstream, treachery in my jaw.

The wall sketched my thoughts in charcoal, painted them
flagrant reds & violent yellows tinged with a darkness I
desired.

Without words for fire we succumbed to original sins that lit up
humid nights like enemy planes, glowworm-green on radar
screens; like manic silent video games; like bombs, ash-
frozen blasts.

I tongued the seam of wallpaper, one strip overlapping another.
Each night my fingers nimble as beaks worked it loose.

We ate roux when we first fell in love, thick spice of hours.

Your mother's children were apple-seeds, arsenic at the core, a
slow & subtle poison. White bits of death in slick teardrops
of life.

We lived in defeated lands with clarified days, red-orange
moments in which our lives glowed like islands: some large

as empires, others solitary jagged rocks that scraped the fickle
sky. Always, something hostile lapped at our shores.

I wore widow white like a pilgrim or a zealot, blazing pure,
believing only in my own strength.

Since pain was alchemical, I wondered if my renaissance in the
rubble would come as victor or victim. Midas-kissed, might I
emerge in a sarcophagus of gold or pyrite?

For this I was punished.

Empire made us monkeys, robbed us of our lips and palates. I
could only say in the crudest way, *behnchod*, sister-fuck. How
I longed for the history of words, of ourselves.

Silence incandesced in my breast. The astronomers discovered
what I knew: All the black holes are our stories, imploded.

Ached for a comrade in arms, in my arms, in my open empty
arms.

Gazed at the white wall to sit zazen, afloat in black robes: mirror,
anchor, screen.

Tasted salt of duty tears, dharma of the good wife, cold gold of
wedding bands, the mangal-sutra's black eyes.

Pain hit me like a lover or a father or a national hero. I thought I
was my only chance for survival. That loneliness.

In moments of grace the sky revealed its cave of silver & we
laughed high up there knowing a whole geography, how to
trace the faults to their origins & forgive.

The walls had strange white accents, echoed between my
eardrums, a percussion of desire.

Even the centuries petrified me.

Headlights beamed warnings. Morse sparkled over asphalt.

In this alphabet of silence I tasted amoebae of heartache
   splitting, multiplying asexual & primitive, a simple goo from
   which our cravings & pairings rise, sticky as solitude.

In echo chambers, canyons, I chanted: *What I need is a new
   family a new recipe is a change of attitude of scenery is a red
   leather jacket a permanent wave is breast surgery is to wave
   goodbye.*

To write: to succumb to the temptation of holding-on, not-
   letting-go.

Accumulation, grasping, delusion of permanence.

With solemn tongue I trace ancient carvings.

My 42 walls make a maze. They call me Minotaur.

Aiyyana Maracle

g>ode to femininity

O Great Goddess of Femininity, how do I transgress thee? Let me count thy ways: first and foremost, one is required to be born with the correct plumbing and appropriate fixtures. Reconstructed and/or customized assemblages installed after birth, quite normally has been grounds for disqualification from this category. Femininity, as a Western construct, with few exceptions, quite normally has not been conferred upon or attributed to NDN (or brown or black women generally, for that matter). Heterosexual femininity, in form and function, quite normally, has not been applicable to women who love women.

Quite likely, I'm guilty of other minor transgressions, but rather than making a big list of them here, let's look at these first few fundamentals. Somewhere mid-century, Western society's medical establishment attempted to address the realities of gender outside of the male-female dichotomy. From the minds of those great good doctors came the decision to pathologize as a psychiatric disorder what we now have come to call transgender or gender variance, a natural phenomenon that occurs throughout all of humanity. First mistake! From here, they declared that the 'cure' for this disorder was intense psychiatric counseling in tandem "with surgical intervention for the most acute cases." Sounds frighteningly close to the recommended course of action leading to a lobotomy, another lovely experiment just coming into vogue about the same time. However, in the case of "gender dysphoria", it is the basis of the psychiatric 'counseling' (and its underlying social philosophy) that needs to come into question, rather than the surgical procedures.

For decades, and to a large degree today, the medicos practicing in the field regarding MTFs felt that these "men" who felt their body was incongruous with their psyche could and should be made over into the image of the ideal woman, physically and mentally. And were they pumped on this: "We can do that! We have the technology! And when it comes to head games and re-organizing psyches, we're tops!" Fortunately, things haven't quite gone according to "the plan." It should be pointed out that when these hypotheses were laid down, circa 1950, the epitome of the ideal Western woman was represented by the staid, heterosexual housewife, standing somewhere behind her husband and surrounded by her white picket fence and 2.5 children. This was the myth that transsexual women were to aspire to, then and now.

Outside of the fashion dilemma this posed, the faulty presuppositions behind this logic generated another conundrum: these "men," in their desire to be women, must naturally be sexually attracted to men. It was incomprehensible to these good doctors that any of these new-found women just might like other women. And yet today, most docs will still try to dissuade their clients from any lesbian notions. Surprise! Ya gotta fight to be a dyke!

In doing my time at Vancouver's gender clinic in the early nineties, I placed myself beyond the good doctors' grasp in declaring myself a Mohawk transformed woman—a woman rooted in her Indigenous ways and cultural practices as old as The People themselves. Throughout most Indigenous cultures, men or women like myself, those who crossed the genders, were accorded respected positions in our societies as special people. We became who we were because we were gifted by the Grandmothers through visions or other means. Our role rather naturally has been mediator between woman and man, and between people and the world of spirit. Our path, our journey, has taken us through these places. We have lived these things; we know; they are part of who we are. Even though the old words to name people like myself may no longer exist in my language, the history of my people led me to term myself a transformed woman of the Haudenosaunee people. These knowledges have been the source of my strength and solace throughout my journey. I assured these good doctors that though I might fit within their European definition of a transsexual, this was hardly all of who I was. For me, these primarily spiritual and emotional connections were sorely missing from the formulas and mis-equations of their outdated, Euro-centric diagnosis and treatment of transsexualism, with its primary focus on the more cosmetic aspects of the journey.

Having said all that, I must confess to having been at some point and for a time quite consumed with certain cosmetic elements. Yet, in coming to woman, there was never any doubt that I was femme. What began as a fashion statement became a journey of discovering all that femme could be for me.

When Aiyyana emerged, she realized that one of her immediate concerns to solve was, "What did she look like?" Over the next few years, this grew into a sometimes embarrassing experiment. She'd always known who she was. But, as she had existed almost four decades inside of "that guy's façade", and seldom had ventured out on her own (then only in *very* private moments), Aiyyana had never really had the opportunity to develop much of a fashion sense. She was occasionally given to pouting over the "unfairness" of "real" women having had literally a lifetime of opportunity to figure out what they should, and perhaps more importantly, should not wear. She learned from her work in theatre and performance art that simple was good. But how did that translate for her fashion-wise? Aiyyana felt sadly and somewhat enviously that maybe she was too large for the frills and lace, or maybe it was just that *they* somehow weren't suited for how *she* was. She was aware that she was drawn to these items, and only slowly admitted that it was probably actually the woman underneath that made these items work so very well for her.

On the street and certainly at the clinic, Aiyyana too often had to wince (and to be honest, sometimes roll her eyes, though she shouldn't have) at consistently seeing these poor dears who followed the clinic's advice, stumbling about in ridiculous costumes that parodied the myth's image, attempting to pass. My gracious, if that is indicative of the level of advice given to these poor souls in their counseling sessions, she felt vindicated in her refusal to attend. Going along, it didn't take much to figure that, as she didn't come from the world of drag queens, and drag was based in parody of woman anyway, that was not an option. She was a woman, after all. Besides, it was an awful lot of work. Not to mention, aesthetically and practically highly inappropriate for her daily life. For a short while, she tried spandex, but that tended to be read as flamboyantly gay. Wrong again.

Eventually Aiyyana came to consider that she was a grandmother and wondered culturally what would be appropriate. She drew on visions from her youth, of her grandmas, her mum, and some of her aunties and older cousins. They were proud urban NDN women riding the crest of a new wave. A two-generation shift from the Rez to cities and towns, trying hard to fit in and survive this European lifestyle. Partly in self-defense, and largely because it suited them, the women of her family tended to be wonderfully dressed in the styles of the day, and honey, femme to the hilt. Watching Aiyyana's mum and her mum's mum, she saw how elegance and dignity looked, with or without the glam. And now Aiyyana was riding the crest of a whole other social shift, thankfully rooted in her past in a way that her mum and grannies had been disallowed from being. So from that point on, it became a matter of extrapolation for her. If these women dressed like that, and approached life like this, then today's equivalent for her would be...

Shopping in Value Village and elsewhere, Aiyyana would stroll past racks of dresses, skirts, blouses, and sweaters, running her hand across the fabrics, only stopping when she'd feel the silks, linens, fine wools, and cottons. Like a couple of her grannies, she got cold easily, and only natural fibres would keep her warm. Invariably, the garments whose touch stopped her in the racks were also the more expensive, finer cuts and hangs, obviously intended for her discriminating wardrobe. Aiyyana's only fashion maxim came from the incomparable Sophia. To paraphrase: "One doesn't follow fashion. It's a question of style. Finding a style that is you, and maintaining it to suit who you are." For the adolescent Aiyyana, Sophia Loren was Hollywood's echo of her own maternal grandmother's sense of glamour with grace. Aiyyana supposed that it must be so, and it seemed to be working for her by the amount of favourable commentary she was beginning to receive on her appearance. She never felt terribly obliged to declare herself as femme, as most everyone else took care of that for her. And, as people are wont to do in their need to box and label things, this assertion of her femme-ness was backed up and proven by her petite partner H, suddenly and without H's knowledge, becoming a butch. It's scary that the first voices to declare this essentially heterosexual woman a lesbian, then a butch, came from women who would regard themselves as feminists. All simply because the person H had come to love could no longer live the pretense of being a man. Aiyyana kindly reminded them that having our identity determined by who our partner is was not part of this Great Struggle for Womanhood.

Anyway, except for the part about her honey being arbitrarily declared a butch, this femme thing suited Aiyyana just fine, and vice-versa. And gee, it's not like she ever expected anyone to refer to her as feminine. She was, after all, still only an Indian woman, and a transformed one at that. It had been a difficult struggle to be seen as woman. Life had clearly shown her that NDN women were still seen as sluttish, squaws, whores, wild, dirty, savagely lustful but with a bunny-like joy at proliferation, exotic, princesses, doe-eyed & docile, tidy, striking, attractive, handsome, occasionally beautiful. But for half a century, she had no memory of ever reading or hearing of an Indian woman described as feminine. Funny the words and attributes the colonizers keep for themselves.

And just what has this femininity devolved into anyway? An instrument in the orchestration of the binary-hetero-mating ritual? A tool for the securing of a husband? Or simply a prop on the stage of heterosexual life? Somewhere along the line, to be feminine became locked into a Snow White persona, so that femininity no longer was the domain of all women, but was attributable to only a certain class of heterosexual women. So, just what is the relationship between femininity and femme? It would be nice to think that in establishing femme as an identity unto itself (a gender perhaps?), and while we are reclaiming language, that it would all somehow contribute to humanizing femininity as again being the collective attributes of *all* women.

As I think about Sophia's attitude, that it's not a question of fashion, but of style, style here is akin to a way of being that is creative, individual, and independent. And that's how femme is: a way of being, born out of a creative individuality unto itself, not dependent on some binary other to identify herself. And for me, there's also this cultural thing, a pride in always presenting yourself to the world as the best you can be in the moment, in body, mind, heart, and spirit.

My transformation to woman has been a conscious and thoughtful process. I was certainly aware that it really still wasn't cool to be a lipstick lesbian in the early 90's when Aiyyana was emerging from her cocoon. But what's a girl to do? Beyond my femme-ness being an innate trait, butch and its uniform just didn't work for me on a lot of levels. In a big way, having spent a quarter-century wearing jeans and heavy boots working as a carpenter, they were the last things I wanted to wear as a woman. (In spite of early in the journey having set a few female hearts aflutter, dressed in some butchy-punk get-up – with lipstick! – in the midst of techie-carpenter work while installing a show. It really wasn't me, but still, it felt pretty nice.) Anyway, here I was – what was I thinking? First, needing to be accepted as woman, then taken as lesbian – one of those lipstick ones – and in the end femme just is, and has her way with me.

I've known from my first memories that I was a girl. I'm uncertain when I knew I was femme. Certainly by the time of my first crush at five years old. But I'm left wondering just when this femme thing entered me. Which really comes first: the femme, or the female?

Vickie Vértiz

Kissing

To block out the sounds of kissing, you turned up the volume on the silver boom box. You pictured British girls in red lipstick, walking through Paris in music videos, their dark sunglasses hiding glances. You undid your ponytail and, like those video girls, tossed your hair at Claudia lying with her arms behind her head on the bottom bunk bed. She pulled you in by the hair. The wall heater hummed and clicked, warming the house and separating you from the living room and your family. Rodney King's grainy face flashed on the television. The freeway where he was surrounded by a halo of bald heads was fifteen miles away from where you were. The waters were rising all around you, but you were not paying attention.

It started like anything else, playing around. You loved your best friend, spending your summers eating pistachio ice cream from the Thrifty's and walking to the video store to rent sexy horror movies starring lesbian vampires. Claudia liked them and that's why you watched.

Then one day Claudia started wrestling with you. It was all right. You were safe at home. She had you in a fake choke hold. You scrambled to get out of it; tickling was your only move. But you liked to win so you tickled more. You were a reed of a girl the color of pilón with wavy hair and barely five feet tall. Claudia weighed 145 pounds, most of it chichi, lonjas, and arms that made the softball land at home plate.

She flipped you over on the beige carpet where you'd watched actresses get chased into windowless rooms. Claudia was pushing your hands away. She let go and came down close to your lips. You laid there panting, smiling from the game. She kissed you softly and afraid.

She said, "I'm sorry. I shouldn't have done that."

You said, "It's okay. I didn't mind."

This was true. You liked it. You were used to saying Yes, had no idea how to said No. You would go along with things to spare people's feelings. She kissed you again and you felt her chapped lips and old braces, the ones her mother was too cheap to get removed even though the teeth were already straight. Because you were not supposed to do this, because you didn't want to hurt her feelings, and because you delighted at the topless women in sheer night gowns of sexy Mexican movies, and if you closed your eyes, Claudia could be one of them. For all these reasons, you made out for three weeks with your best friend.

You made sure no hickies were on exposed body parts. Claudia was doing all the work, biting your skin into magenta roses. In the afternoons after your honors English homework was done, you'd lock the door to the family bedroom or in the bedroom Claudia shared with her mom. You would hide under Disney cartoon bedsheets kissing until your faces hurt. You liked the biting, the licking of your small breasts. But you were hoping the sex would feel better. You'd been masturbating since you were twelve to a stockpile of made up porno in your brain and knew enough to know Claudia didn't know shit about it. When her fingers found your clit, they just poked around like when you brushed your teeth with your fingers when you went camping. You faked orgasms once the clumsy sliding around got repetitive. At least she had short nails.

By the second week of making out, you got brave. You put your mouth on her C cups, feeling up around the pale folds of skin. Claudia's cotton bra fabric cut into her sides, tender where the bra dug into her. You tried to put your hand inside her black bikini panties, but she didn't let you. You didn't want to, but you were supposed to. You didn't try it again because you didn't have to: you were getting all the attention.

Around your family, you thought you were acting normal, but your dad saw you hanging close to Claudia. From behind his black '68 Impala, he saw Claudia kiss your hand, then ride off on her bike after she asked you to be her girlfriend. He shook his head; he could see you were turning out just like him—women throwing themselves at you in broad daylight. He did not tell your mom about what he saw. Once she'd left, he told you, "Jenny, be careful with that girl, mija. She's not who you think."

You said, "Whatever, Dad. Don't worry about it." You waved off his fourth grade education. You didn't think about what it meant that he said this. You thought you knew best.

That night, your right ear was sore from pressing to the receiver.

"I think I'm in love with my best friend," Claudia whispered into the phone. "I mean, not in love, you know..."

"Don't worry," you assured her. "I was reading *Sassy* and this article said it's totally normal for girls to have feelings for their best friends."

"Are you sure?" said Claudia. "It's not weird or anything?"

"No, silly," you said. "You're fine."

She sighed and you could tell she felt better. You looked at your clean, squared nails, feeling like an expert at matters of the heart. You were not concerned because you did not think about going to prom with her or having her babies. You did not yearn for her. Claudia did not notice your calm. She was too worried about what kissing you said about her.

During those weeks it rained so much that the L.A. River was full. Walking back to your house from Claudia's, you went two blocks up Gage Avenue to the river and watched from the bridge, its low concrete railing the only thing keeping you from the froth kissing the lip of the river bed. It moved so hurriedly that you pictured the river knocking open the front door of your house, pouring in through the windows after jumping the freeway wall. The dirty water would come in so fast that your family and belongings would not be able to escape, your bodies floating like dead goldfish. You pulled Claudia away from the rail and said, "That's enough."

The boombox was not loud enough to hear from the kitchen. Your house was a single bedroom bungalow built in the 1940s. There was a heater in the wall with slits you could see through. The wall was shared by the family's bedroom and the living room, the bedroom where your whole family slept. The queen bed was where you parents slept. You and your brother split the bunk beds.

Your mom was busy frying chile and garlic. Two televisions were on, one playing novelas, the other cartoons for your brother in the living room. When you girls had walked in, she eyed Claudia. She didn't like that Claudia couldn't speak Spanish; such a liar, she thought.

Your radio was playing muted electronic keyboards. You were topless, still wearing white denim shorts. Claudia was fully clothed, lying with you in the bottom bunk. She was holding you by the waist, talking about renting the latest *Faces of Death* movie that weekend.

Your mother needed you to buy fideo at the store. She was not ashamed to see what you were doing with the door closed. Your brother was busy with his two He-man toys and second-hand Legos. She turned off the flame and walked the few steps into the living room. She peeked through the grate in the wall heater.

She saw your bare back facing her, and Claudia's arms around you.

"Open the door!" She yanked the knob so hard it almost came off. Claudia sat up, throwing you a green T-shirt to wear. You had no plan. You thought you'd get away with being this free.

You opened the door to a charging bull. She slapped you once across the face. She shook you, demanded to know what you were doing. Claudia rubbed her hands together and stared at the floor. She did not speak Spanish and could not answer your mother when she asked questions. You moved out to the hallway to plead insanity.

"This is the only time we've done it," you cried. "We promise never to do it again." Your brother gathered his toys and went outside to play. He was used to people fighting; the yard was the only place to go. Claudia passed you and sat on the living room couch, sensing it would be a bad move to leave, the garlic and chile in the air like mace. Your mother walked in circles in the living room, her chubby brown hands cutting the air.

"You can't hang out alone together anymore! If Claudia

comes over, you have to sit out where everyone can see you." You translated this to Claudia. She nodded. You thought you were making progress.

"You need to go home," said your mom. Claudia left, and you went after her, saying you'd call later. "No, dummy. Go talk to your mom. Don't call me tonight," she said.

You went back in and repeated yourself. Your mom said, "You're not supposed to do that with girls," and wiped her eyes. You said it didn't mean anything about you. You convinced yourself that your mom, who was raised on a ranch, had also read that *Sassy* article. Your mom agreed to let Claudia come over sometimes. You said okay and thought you'd won. But then she said, "I have to talk with her mother." You jumped in front of the phone. "No, mami," you said. "Please not right now."

She backed away but you wondered how long you had before shit went down with Claudia's mom. You were afraid of her over-powdered face, her meaty hands strong as a man's. Claudia's mother frequently beat the shit out of her when they argued. Your mom marched out to buy pasta for dinner and took your brother.

Your mothers had never met and didn't speak the same language. They wouldn't need big words to punish their daughters.

The next day, the rain stopped.

You met Claudia during nutrition. "Your mom called my house late last night," said Claudia. She turned her face and a bruise like dirt colored her jaw. "Don't call my house until things get better."

"I'm not sorry for what we did," you said. Fuck everyone, you thought.

"I am," she said. "You don't have to deal with my mom. I gotta go, kid."

She did not look back at you. What would you do without her? She was all of your time. The whole neighborhood would know what happened. You walked around school worse than a loner, a gay loner who didn't think she was gay at all.

TC Tolbert

Vena Amoris

I'm on a relatively small plane on my way to Denver. I'm in the window seat. There is no middle, just the guy in the aisle seat whose elbow keeps grazing my arm. We're both white men. He's 6'1, maybe, 6'2, muscular. I'm 5'8, 150. He is not unkind. I'm bad at this sort of thing but I'd say he's in the neighborhood of 220 pounds. Right away, he put the armrest down and got comfortable. He's sleeping now or trying to. Elbows outnumber armrests. We are close but we are not intimate. Presumably we are meant to negotiate the space.

Whenever I do *Made for Flight,* I visit classrooms, gay-straight alliances, and youth centers and talk about trans identities, violence, how to be an ally. We make a kite for each trans woman who has been murdered during the year. We walk with those kites during the All Souls Procession in Tucson. I am constantly saying these words*: two trans women are murdered each month here in the US. A trans woman (usually a trans woman of color) is murdered every other day worldwide.* Does saying this change anything for trans women? What does it mean to be complicit? When Janet Mock says, *Every time there is a trans woman of color in the media, she's getting killed. It wrecks our souls.* To whom or what is she pointing? Do the dead women give a goddamn about all of those kites?

It is on the plane that I realize how long it's been since I've felt willingly vulnerable. In "A Brief for the Defense," Jack Gilbert says, "We must risk delight. We can do without pleasure, not delight." I went to a performance of John Cage's *Sonatas and Interludes* last night because my heart is absolutely desperate for surprise.

I grew up in a family (and culture) that treated those closest with the most utter contempt. The idea that intimates pose the biggest emotional and physical threats isn't entirely far fetched. Statistically speaking, it's like Nicholas Christakis and James Fowler say in *Connected*, "If you want to know who might take your life, just look at the people around you." Still, these are the same people who are bound to save your life. Although they are undoubtedly related, sometimes I worry much less about politics and hate crimes than I do about what we agree to call love. Self-loathing, continual justification for bad partner behavior, far more struggle than joy. A fear of scarcity. I see it because I know it. An epidemic among women, trans folks, and queers. I'm looking for a new story about love.

I was at a wedding the other day—a hybrid Jewish and Christian ceremony—and the rabbi said that in Jewish tradition the wedding ring is initially placed on the index finger because an artery runs to the tip of the finger we point with—the one that says "you, this, now, here"—carrying blood directly from the heart. In this way we reveal more about ourselves by what we point to (or away from) than we ever could by saying how we feel.

I went to the John Cage performance last night for the same reason I get on an airplane instead of driving, which is the same reason I eat in public even though it would be cheaper to have the same meal at home. Amy said intimacy isn't about sharing our worst stories, it's about sharing the stories that come up. Julia said Halloween is the only American holiday that depends on interacting with others across (and beyond our own) identity categories in an exuberant gesture of good faith. Who are the monsters, really? What do we have to suspend in order to experiment with trust?

When my Sam put his hand on my shoulder as he was walking by, it was a kindness rarely offered between men. I know that now because I'm a man. I needed his hand. Even if I am scared of being touched.

TC Tolbert

Buttress

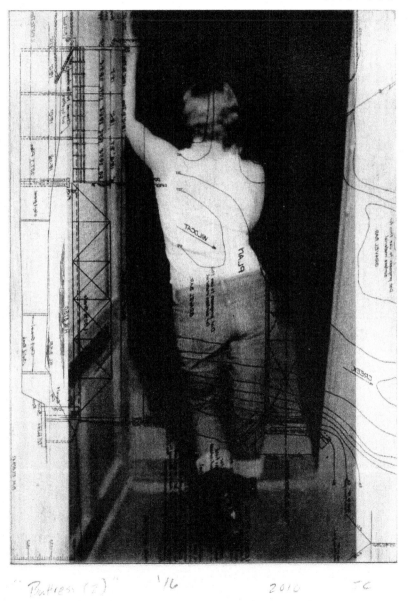

Hannah J Stein

Polished Glass

I couldn't believe that I was late for the interview. After months of unemployment, I was appalled to find myself now sprinting down the busy sidewalk, desperately trying to size up which of these massive shining buildings was the tallest in Minnesota. It didn't help my mood that I was wearing a suit and tie. Many of my fellow pedestrians gave me strange looks—most likely due to my velocity, or lack of a good Midwestern blob coat in the February winter—and my mind raced as to whether my current presentation as a "typical young male business professional" was being undone by my unusually long hair or my larger-than-your-average-male chest. The emotional side-effects of the micronized estradiol I was taking weren't exactly helping me stay calm as I ran, my reflection flickering through the various storefront windows.

To be fair, the 18 bus had been late. To be honest, I had also been late. I had spent far too long trying to rub salt stains off my old black shoes, sighing at the mirror in the suit I had borrowed from my friend, wondering if I was a sell-out to "The Man." Despite the countless evils of soulless corporatism, money does indeed makes the world go 'round, and my sheer lack of it had resulted in piles of unpaid medical bills, late rent payments, and a dwindling food supply. On the bus ride to downtown, I had investigated this apartment sales company on my cracked phone screen. Scrolling past the search results of blogs that decried their predatory practices, I landed on the flashy website for the gleaming new apartment complex that they were building. High end luxury, right in the middle of downtown. They were to include an indoor dog park, pet spa, human spa, shops...

I remember sitting in the office of the staffing agency who had found this interview for me. Their glass walls peered out into a central interior courtyard, providing an unsettling view of the offices directly above and below it. I hadn't been on hormones very long at that point, and my hair was more typical for a male my age. It was, however, unkempt, because I had just desperately run to make that appointment as well. That particular maniacal sprint (while more justified by the 10 bus absolutely failing to arrive at all) had been far worse; the bitter wind blew ice crystals and snow from rooftops into my face, turning it painfully red as I ran in another ill fitting suit to get to another strange building that I had never been to before.

Was this an activity I did frequently? I felt like some trapped, unemployed animal, scurrying through a grid of tall buildings, perpetually at the mercy of ephemeral figures in expensive clothes who all seemed to share a good laugh at my socio-economic standing. These were the people who walked above in the skyways, rather than upon the salt-splotched concrete; mythical overlords from the land of parking passes and finance management.

And now, I seemed to be in the heart of their world. Out of breath and wheezing, I staggered into the building lobby and began to scan a nearby directory of businesses for the company's office location. The info map had nothing helpful to offer me, and I worried that I had somehow managed to choose the wrong "tallest building in Minnesota." I ran up escalators, sought the advice of strangers. I was officially late.

I paced around the lobby beneath an indoor waterfall that fell from several stories into a public seating area, the benches and tables corralled by skinny little trees in large planters. The fellow who was theoretically supposed to interview me hadn't picked up the phone, and I left an embarrassing voice mail in which I confidently said that I now knew where I was going and would be there soon. I then decided to ask the security guards for help.

We flipped through the paper catalog of every company who rented an office in all fifty-five floors of the tower. As I was wringing my hands, one of the guards looked straight ahead and noticed a glitzy sign on the wall of a glass kiosk that referenced the company I so desperately hunted... directly in the center of the atrium. "You ran past it a bunch there, didn't ya?" he laughed. Thanking them, I awkwardly scampered over to the booth, racking my brain for excuses.

Nobody was there, and the doors were locked. This miniature office structure had no ceiling, opening directly into the lobby (which I had just learned was called the "Crystal Court"). A few sleek, white stools seemed to float above the flawless hardwood floor. All the walls were glass, and covered in advertisements that evoked green leaves and expensive graphic design. I stood there staring into the fishbowl office, weakly jostling the silver door handle. I had been less than ten minutes late... had they really given up on me that quickly?

"Excuse me," said a voice startlingly close to the back of my head, "do you work here?" I whirled around to see a suited man with a coffee peering at the ads. "Um, no... I mean... not yet!" I nervously smiled. We made small talk about how these places looked slick, would probably take a while to be built. As he strolled away, my self-confidence swelled to realize that in his eyes, I looked professional enough to work there. Apparently all you need to look like an apartment salesman is a suit and a folder, even if the latter only contains a few copies of your resume. Mine were still warm from the ten-cent printer in the library.

I waited for a good long while, pacing back and forth. To my disbelief, two more people came up to ask me about the apartments. Despite the immense internal distress that I had squandered this interview (and extreme discomfort in the suit), I managed to make cheerful small talk about my job search with these businessmen. I gave no indication that the moment they left I would return to the task of fruitlessly redialing the same monotone voicemail in a panicked whir of button mashing. The air was irritatingly filled with calm, professional chatter and the gentle splashing of the controlled waterfall. Getting desperate, I returned to the security guards and asked if they could look through the directory again, in the hopes that there was "like, a physical office somewhere on the fortieth floor or something," as opposed to this seemingly abandoned kiosk.

As they searched the database to no avail, I turned to notice someone standing outside the mini-office with a cell phone. Throwing a thanks over my shoulder, I ran out to the Crystal Court to greet this man. With an excited hello, I inquired as to whether he was the one who was supposed to interview me. Busy on his cell phone, he mouthed the word "no." Perhaps I should have figured by his casual clothing, as the only thing I knew about the interviewer was that he liked men's fashion. Growing agitated with this whole affair, I called their national corporate headquarters. After being told by a secretary that I would be patched through to the Minneapolis regional manager, I had been promptly hung up on. After more than half an hour spent waiting, I stared blankly out into the eerily spotless space as my resentment acquired that bitter flavor of sullen anger.

At that very moment, a lanky bearded man sauntered up next to me and asked, "How much those pads go for?" Without thinking, I spouted off some of the rates I remembered from the rental website. While the other people who had approached me had been businessmen, this guy was dressed in a shabby hoodie and sported a shock of gray hair. His untidy eyebrows seemed to spring forth from the droop of his wrinkled eyelids. As he asked more questions, I decided it couldn't hurt to try my hand at talking up these luxury apartments that neither of us could probably ever afford in our wildest dreams. What would I care if I inadvertently lost them a potential customer? They had wasted a great deal of my time and caused me to compromise my self-respect for no reason. "You work here?" the man asked.

"Yes," I responded in my best impression of a manly salesman voice. I tried to cook up some self-assuredness with a splash of bro. This man asked about the location and I made up a completely false address on the spot, delivering it confidently with a nod of my chin. LEED certified? Of course. Utilities included? "It's a long decision process, but between you and me? Most likely." He wanted to see a pamphlet. Clenching my jaw muscles, I told him just how irritated I was that the locksmith hadn't yet arrived to let us in. "You see?" I said, jostling the handle to show my annoyance. "How am I supposed to do business when we can't get into the office?" The man shook his head.

"You're losing buyers," he informed me, leaning in. "You know how many lawyers walk through here every day?"

I sighed and nodded. "The most frustrating thing," I confided to my client, "is that the office doesn't even have a ceiling! I mean we're heartbreakingly close, why not jump the walls, get inside and unlock it that way?"

The man chuckled at my exasperation. "That's not how it's done in the Crystal Court." He informed me he would be over in the seating area to return after his lunch.

I had just made my first sales pitch for an apartment complex. I felt a little exhilarated, and yet surprised by how easy it had been. After all, I was already acting in the role of "man;" why not add another layer to my performance? Inwardly chirpy, I realized I heard laughter coming from my right. It was the young man who had been standing nearby with a cell phone. He had watched our entire dialogue and was now approaching me. I nervously smiled back, suddenly wondering if this whole interaction had been a set-up, some kind of test.

At that very moment, the office director also approached me from the escalators. Apologizing for the delay, she explained that her co-worker had accidentally scheduled me for an interview on the next day instead. She asked if I could wait just a moment, and then, to my horror, she turned to greet cell phone guy. They went inside the office and sat at a table while I uncomfortably stood outside the glass walls, trying simultaneously not to look inside at their interaction and somehow hear what they were talking about. I couldn't hear a word. Feeling a bit creepy lurking a few feet from them in plain sight, I decided to stroll around the complex. Examining the immaculately pruned foliage, I pondered that they had a relatively strange life compared to most other black olive trees, their existence spent locked away in this untarnished tower in the Midwestern United States.

She returned later to apologize again, gave me a business card and a pat on the back. I hoped she didn't feel the straps of my tight camisole through the suit padding. All things considered, I had lucked out; my bus transfer still hadn't expired so I didn't need to use the last of my quarters to get home. The next day's interview went well (I knew where I was going and arrived early), but ultimately I didn't get that job. I will never know if it had anything to do with the fact that I wildly misinformed one of their potential customers.

Weeks later I was hired by a Lebanese deli within walking distance from my house. Winter is disappearing now, and the trees are growing green with spring. The warm sun has found me wearing earrings, makeup, and whatever clothing I choose to work. My new license features an "F" aside the gender marker, and my long haired portrait smiles giddily from the bendy plastic card. My pronouns are accepted by everyone from school friends to my grandpa.

The restaurant reaches peak hours at midday, when the nearby businesspeople pile in to savor their lunch breaks. As I serve them gyros, I often think about how troublingly easy it was for me to deceive with nothing more than a suit and some strong wording. Food service may not be as lucrative as a job in sales, but it very much operates in reality. The menu lists the name, ingredients, and price of every dish. If any of this Mediterranean cuisine falls to the floor, it is easily swept up. When people leave smudges with their fingertips, I break out the Windex.

Every weekday I find myself polishing the surfaces at a leisurely pace as the radio shuffles through a playlist of love songs. Whatever the future holds, I am comforted to know that when I eventually enter my long term career, it will be as myself. I am also fairly certain it won't involve luxury apartments. For now, I clean the deli case, simultaneously confining and presenting only salads, pastas, and ripe olives.

Dane Slutzky

Birthright

"Aliyah,"the Hebrew school teacher told us
"means to rise up, ascend."
It would feel romantic
Swapping temperate apples
For arid figs and dates.
I have made decisions based on root words,
etymology. It helps to chant
familiar rhythms,
fall into deep grooves worn
by ritual. Now I hear ascend
and see cranes and excavators
poised over the skyline, rusting vultures.
Paving the desert, high rises
for the holy land. All those new people
need somewhere to live.

Moon Flower

Arizona F/law

I'm on a Mexican ra - dio   I'm on a Mexican   W-O-Oh ra – dio

Tohono O'odham   Hopi   Navajo

rodeo   border patrol
frijoleros uniformed

crossin
Indios

founding forefathers
armoured dogs

wrought
terror

                                        corralled
                                        disemboweled

                                        brown bodies
                                        sanctioned ovaries

        now   SB1070

                                majority becomes minority
                                minority becomes majority

soaped mouths
Won't Stop
Revolution

incarceration
Won't Stop
Precious Knowledge

reservation plots
Won't Stop
Sovereignty

Love for people
    peyotzin flower
    Marmon Silko *Ceremony*

        nopal thorns > patriotism
                        Tonantzin overthrows   Washington

I'm on a M–E–X-I–C–A Radio and (sound of dj scratching)

        I'm gonna knock you out, mama said knock you out
            I'm gonna knock you out, Mama SAID
                K–N–O–C-K   Y–O-U   OOOO–U–T!

Joy Ladin

Passing Through Security

They ma'am me at the airport. Fail to detect
explosive bits of gender:
Adam's apple, shoulder width, stubble,
none-of-your-business,
which thank God I don't have to say
because my voice, in anger,
might give me away.
It's official: I am what I say.
Today.

Joy Ladin

Mail for Mr. Jay

still arrives day after day
wherever I move
whatever I say
the man I was won't go away
Not much left of Mr. Jay
Credit card offers exhausted kindness
an impression in cushions
a key whose lock's been changed
Have a cookie Mr. Jay
a crumb of sweetness
a moment without pain
There are toys on the floor why don't you play
one of those games
your children outgrew
You're outgrown too
but just the same
an eraser
that can't be erased
no matter how much I change or blame
you for sticking me with that stupid name
this battered face
these lines that epitaph my forehead
which is after all your grave:
Here lie the remains of Mr. Jay
who confused love with shame
bit his fingernails longed to be good
discovered 12,761 conjugations
of the verb "to wait"

survived without breathing from the moment of birth
to this very day
memento mori reminding all who pass
it's time to go out and play

thokozane minah

Black, Liquid, Fluid

Between churches, libraries, stages and the bedrooms of lovers, I have undergone various exhilarating and harrowing transformations. Always Black, always adapting like liquid, forever evolving; fluid. I am Ink. And I am sacred. This is my story.

I came into being behind the walls of the infamous Johannesburg General Hospital in inner-city Joburg, South Africa, in 1992. I was not entirely planned, not particularly wanted, but there I was, leaving an indelible mark already, on the lives of my young, then unmarried, Christian parents. I went from being a regular baby—unclaimed by any gods, not affiliated with any institutions—to being baptized Christian at the age of two inside the canvas walls of the church's tent. I was a life-long financial burden to a couple who didn't believe in abortions or raising children out of wedlock, forcing them to marry when neither of them was ready for that, or for me. My baptism signified a covenant with their Christian God; a soul won over and dedicated to the Lord's purpose. And possibly a plea for forgiveness for having a child before marriage. Four deep cuts around my infantile belly-button with a sterilized razor marked my ancestors' reception of my existence.

The same canvas flaps also bore witness to my first beating as a three-year-old on the morning of my kid brother's birthday. After a church service, during which I had played in the parking lot with a homeless child, my father used his belt to punish me for losing a brand new lunch box and juice bottle. I had shared that day's lunch with my new found friend in the parking lot. The entire congregation of departing church goers witnessed my hiding; my first experience of humiliation. And later that canvas saw the early introduction of my young brown body to sexual desire expressed by an older boy I knew then only by the name Joseph; my older "brother" not through blood or any kind of genetic lineage, but through Christ, an older boy who went to church with us, whom my mother helped put through school. He found me playing on my own in a sea of empty church chairs, all silently watching as he led me towards a concrete table-like structure built for the camera-men and sound engineers and raped me on the church floor. He would be the first but not the last. The same church will show you how despite all of that early trauma, my young self persevered. All I knew how to do was adapt.

I learned to expect the horror that awaited behind every pair of adult legs, but also learned how to push past that fear when what was required of me was a sharing of my gifts and talents. The church stage would become my first taste of empowerment. Young, Black, liquid, adaptive kid singing and reciting poetry bringing all the damn grown-ups to tears before God. I would hear my voice and be pleased with the sounds I made, see the looks of awe and pleasure in the eyes of the audience and know that I was doing something good; that I can't have been "all bad".

It was clear to me in those moments that I was sacred. I was a young child who bore gifts from the gods that could make people smile, make people cry, make people stand up and clap their hands for me.

I am written also into the walls of a house in a good neighborhood gone bad. Where I received my longest beating yet. In the wooden-floored study a branch was stripped naked of all its leaves, leaving only thorns on a green stem, welts on grazed bleeding brown skin. This house was also the place I first decided to play around with the concept of gender. I would conjure up dozens of fictitious scenarios and turn them into "games" I'd play or "movies" I'd perform for my siblings, sometimes playing characters outside of my gender, sometimes even taking on said characters when the games and movies had ended. Fluidity oozed out of my sometimes short and natural, sometimes long and straightened hair, out of and through a fat ambiguous body and an imagination that seemed to know no bounds regarding who it allowed me to be.

"Is that a boy or a girl?"

This was the whisper that echoed through the walls of the school hall as I strutted about playing Danny from *Grease* on stage in front of the parents of the kids who bullied me. The kids who teased, punched, and pinched me in the school's darkened hallways and sunny playground. The kids who didn't believe me when I announced that I was raped. The kids whose disbelief caused me to keep quiet about all the other shit that happened; the times in the cars that took me home from school when transport drivers would slip their hands beneath my school skirt and rub at my thighs and underwear; being chased around by boys who fancied me and forced themselves on me in clumsy, terribly wet non-consensual kisses.

But I am Ink. And I am sacred. I leave a mark on the memories of those who come into contact with me. I am permanent; not even the entitled, invasive sexual assault, violent beatings, or molestation can wipe me out.

Catholic high school hallways and chapels bore witness to the end of my days as a victim of bullying and violence and the beginning of my days as someone who fought back. Until the day the pavement bore the brunt of a bottle broken for the purpose of a senseless fight that ended before it had even begun. With me standing heaving, panting, my fingers cut and bruised by the broken green glass bottle, my face flushed hot with the embarrassment of the silent reprimand I felt emanating from the school yard walls.

Those same school yard walls and the walls of the washed-out chapels within them housed the first fledgling surges of my complex sexuality. A boyfriend whose body reminded me too much

of past traumas; who didn't coerce sex from me, but instead pummeled his fists into my body, frustrated that he wasn't getting what he was "entitled" to in that relationship. A girlfriend who was at first a best friend but became my "aha, I am a lesbian," moment, which turned into "I don't really remember the last time I actually wanted to have sex with you and didn't feel pressured or coerced into doing so." How even within those relationships carried out mostly in secret stairwells and abandoned confession rooms, my fluidity subtly revealed itself when my clothing—I donned my winter pants, which were baggy, and bold hairdos (I'd shave all of my hair off on a whim)—suggested the presence of a masculine energy which seemed sinister to those two serious lovers. But intrigued the many younger babes I would have shorter, sweeter affairs with. Babes who'd comment, "You'd be the perfect guy, Mercy."
And maybe in some ways, I was.

The library in that Catholic high school still carries the memory of me buried in there the other 70% of my high school life: angst-filled, isolated, too heavy and complex for my own good, grappling with a darkness I couldn't always fully understand but which I knew had been present since I was ten. I read more than I breathed. I wrote too. Constantly. Letters. Manuscripts. Short stories. I filled out diaries and discarded them. The library saw all of this. It witnessed me drawing and painting too. There is so much of me spilled and smeared across the walls of that high school and its classrooms and chapels. So much of me that was tentative in some instances, wild and bursting forth in others, tantalized and intoxicated by the promise of freedom that lay on the other side of teenagehood. On the outside of my mother's house.

I am Ink. And I am sacred.

I apply for a prestigious public university's law school. I don't know what the fuck I am doing there. I don't love law and law doesn't love me. My deepest fears and insecurities about academia and my future are birthed in lecture halls. Along with my distaste for the ways in which intellectualism consistently erases and pathologizes me. Black, liquid, and fluid as I am. Artistic, depressed, gay. It isn't all bad though. Universities have gay societies. I have a family of fellow rainbow babies who take me in on the condition that I have an identity that resembles theirs. The Black and liquid take over first. I am surrounded by other Black people with their own ideas about identity, and I am liquid so I adapt and allow them to mold me into a version of myself that best suits their agenda.

I am quiet about my atheism. I am quiet about my sexual fluidity. My gender fluidity. I have yet to fully understand what it means to be Ink. To be sacred.

Lecture halls and res rooms and student accommodation apartments see me blossom sexually. Black and liquid and gay. And free. Until four o' clock when my momma picks me up and takes me back home. Where the beatings have stopped and been replaced by insults, by psychological warfare. And I have a steady supply of alcohol stashed away in various parts of my bedroom, where the only indicator that I am gay is a rainbow-colored shoe string tied around the handle of one of my closets doors. A less permanent indicator of my gayness is the secret presence of white lovers. One, a temporary fling, weed-infused and laced with dancing, musing on the country's state of affairs and brief sexual encounters whenever I sneak over to her house next door in the absence of our families. The other, more volatile and silently sinister; a drawn-out relationship with a girl I introduce to my mother as my "new best friend", who is seemingly sweet at first but turns out to have very little regard for my agency or bodily integrity; another situation in which my body belongs more to another than to me.

And in the midst of it all I am occupying a virtual space, with virtual walls, allowing myself to spill forth onto a platform that is slightly more freeing. The internet opens itself up to me and without knowing it, with every Facebook post and rant and picture that I share, I begin writing myself into existence.

I am learning how the depth and fluidity of my being makes me like Ink. How I am worthy of taking up space, of self-determination, because I am sacred.

A new library houses me in that university. The gay library. Home to a collection of roughly 200 queer texts. I don't know what queer means until I enter this place. Where more than just political indignation is awakened. Where that early on fluidity seeps out from my past and onto the walls of that tiny closed up space. Constant dialogue about identity, sexuality, and gender expression reminds me of my childhood experimentation with gender expression, freeing me up to change the way I present through clothing, to explore a myriad of labels and identification markers used by us gender-variant children the world over. In this library are two shelves, a table to drink coffee, and thousands of DVDs (all 6 seasons of *The L Word*, hundreds of popular movie titles from Charlize Theron's *Monster* to Hilary Swank's *Boys Don't Cry*) and videos (seasons of *Queer As Folk*, numerous documentaries capturing Pride celebrations in different parts of Africa during the 90's). I grow thick and tangible within the walls of that library. Every book (some more significantly than others, namely *Stone Butch Blues* by Leslie Feinberg, Staceyann Chin's *The Other Side of Paradise*) DVD, and conversation filling me up, turning me into a substance that matters, a deliberate and conscious entity.

And there are break-ups and break-downs which follow, seemingly as a result of a more controlled course of my Black, liquid, fluid self. People are not accustomed to a me that is written into spaces with purpose. And when many of these spaces that house me propel me to relive some of the trauma of my past by triggering memories of rejection, rumor, hostility, I find refuge one last time in another place within that university. Ostracized and isolated once more I turn to computer labs as a sanctuary for my complex self. I find connection, solace, family even across the plains of the cyber sphere.

I spend my mornings on YouTube, studiously watching the

journeys of trans* folks of all genders as they determine themselves; my lunch breaks are spent pouring over blogs written by queer and trans* people of color who introduce me to new ways of writing my existence. Tumblr, Blogspot, Wordpress accounts detailing, through imagery and writing, the beauty of human journeys into the infinite possibilities of gender and sexuality. Taking in the vastness of existence and the human experience cementes my growing sense of sacredness. Reading and watching those blogs and YouTube channels, respectively, which are sometimes three, four, seven years old when I discover them, become a revelation: it is possible to be permanent, like Ink. I begin to write my own blogs to immortalize my existence.

I am Ink. And I am sacred.

I am Black, liquid and fluid. I am an African of Zulu/Swati/Ndebele descent, an urban baby with a restless soul so displaced in white Jewish South African suburbia. I am a pansexual genderqueer boi, masculine of center and a seeker of the genderqueer spirit that roams the multiverse in search of its children, whom it knows by name. I am Ink that has been written on thousands of diary and journal pages, inscribed onto dozens of love letters, identification documents marking the reality of my existence, and a myriad of virtual platforms in cyber space. I am written and that is how I have been able to uncover and make sense of my identity, how I have been able to overcome trauma and be buoyed by triumph. I am deeply anchored in the knowledge of my sacredness and even as I revisit the places of my past, driving past the old church tent, my old schools, interacting with my remaining parent, I am no longer apologetic about the ways I take up space. When someone remembers me, whether they have loved or hurt me, and shows that recognition when they meet me on the street, I feel myself swelling with the depth of my significance, the indelible mark I have left in all of the places I have been written into.

Alfonzo Moret

Traveling The Limbo

India Inks, pencil, and acrylic paints, 22 1/2 x 34 1/2

This painting is rather complex. It speaks of life after death, and the path one has to follow in order to reach the other side. When I was eleven years of age, my biological father died; he was shot to death by the LAPD. I only met him twice in my life; the second time was at his funeral. I was told he was a troubled artist, who had talent and a drug habit. Later that year while at swimming class, someone thought I knew how to swim, so he pushed me into the pool. I sank like a stone to the bottom and lay there looking up at the children having fun. Then suddenly I was out of the pool looking down at my body, in the deep blue waters below, thinking, "So this is how I die?" I traveled so high I could see the earth, pulled by a silver cord protruding from my belly button. Then I entered this golden tunnel filled with bright blue colored light; from inside it looked like a cornucopia.

When I reached the end I was surrounded with loving ancestors, standing on clouds. Their faces were not clear, but their voices I recognized; they informed me it wasn't my time and I had to return to my body on earth. I never got the chance to see my father or ask if he was here. Then with a gentle push I fell painfully back into my body. When I awoke they all cheered, saying, "He's alive!! You were dead, but now you are alive!"

deborah brandon

XI. Jellyfish Chandelier

I unfolded when he wasn't looking. If I wanted my boy to flush with a firm belief, I would need to move the hamper.

My sister pushed him from the sky. He had his dark flight and a crater to cradle him. The clearest view showed artificial hearts bleating across the sky then the flatline horizon, gaping it.

So then Sparrow returned the scorpion. I lost my immunity in one fell swoop. I knew what I could not carry.

I lay on the bed while he fussed to fit himself – a red wheel – to my neck. I tongued incomprehensible wine into his mouth. He took the venom into another room.

I put the kettle on. A relief to find the walls blue again.

deborah brandon

XIV. what breath

i wake at six and place tiny boats
across her belly   she is phosphorescence
lights corrode each other only briefly

you, swift fawn, your face is snow,

my gilded one   lips pressed into
parchment   walls.
sand's weight   it pours
through   the window
i kiss you   i kiss you
against & into   against & into

a voyage subsisting on bones.

deborah brandon

XXII. I See Its Shadow But Not the Bird

Sparrow takes the sugar, and also the imitation, into his hands and turns them.

He says: When I was a little girl, I lived in a house that had a wall. All the goldfish had names. In the first year I grew out of my doll and took to rabbits. In the night, Mother. The door open to a false season.

> A bird taps the window behind my head. If I turn, it will startle. How do I silence the sound of threatened exit or resigned return? How will I learn their language, flying?

Sparrow, I say. You're not safe; you're in the sea. They are all in their houses with nobody talking. They are all inside doors. I love—

Now he is leaving. The linoleum stair snuffs silent his heels, but the sidewalk won't. I watch Sparrow's lamp. A nest rolls beyond him, over the road.

deborah brandon

XXIV. Phoenix

I must leave my father's house without ants following. His floor is earth, impossible to tread without trace. He is untraceable; he is departed.

First, I prepare the walls for collapse. Pull fittings from sockets to put an end to their charges. Unwrap cords from my wrists. Wrestle a hinge in the grave, milky with dust motes.

I must cause a helicopter to rise if I will find him. I wait motionless with the radio in my hand, ready to signal.

At long last the ceiling begins its give.

The earth that is father: roots in a dry swamp. I twist them into hoops. No one will raise a finger, let alone a fist. This time, static creeps up the beanstalk. One single certainty.

Ants bless my feet. And I fear the helicopter's methods. My father's air stands here, milling his cells into snow, urged into sky for safety.

Patricia Powell

Your Own Heart

It is a dark night. A man comes to the door and rings the bell. It is late. She wakes. Is that really the bell? There is a pounding on the door and in her heart too a pounding. The dog next door is barking and barking. She gets up from underneath the blankets - it's freezing in the house. She drags an extra shirt over her head and moves quickly up the stairs. Who could it be? The bell is still ringing; she puts on the light. Who is it? She peers through the tiny hole; she makes out no one. There is no voice, just the insistent ringing. Lights come on next door. The neighbor yells at the dog. Enough already, quiet down! She doesn't know who is at the door; she is right there; it's ringing and ringing. Finally she grabs a knife from the kitchen; she grabs a hammer. Okay, she cries. Her arms are shaking. She flings opens the door. Yes!

A man enters. A man she can only see from the periphery of her vision; if she stares too hard she doesn't see him, or if she stares head on; but if she looks off to the side she can see him. There is a child too, a boy, and they walk in together. They seem cold; they are shivering. It's been raining, but they're not wet. They are wearing black suits and sparkling white shirts and real skinny black ties. They walk past her and head into the living room. They don't say hi, good night, or thank you. They recline on the sofa; they ease off their shoes.

She knows she is to make something warm, tea perhaps, something sweetened for the boy, and for him, something black and strong. She looks out briefly into the darkness and then locks the door behind her. In the kitchen she makes tea, sweetens it with honey, hands it to the boy who is fast asleep. She has to pry him awake and waits so he takes it carefully in both hands. She just had the white couch cleaned. If he stains it there will be hell to pay.

The man looks at her warily.

I don't work for you, she says.

Still she brings him coffee; he sips it slowly, slurping on the mug.

It's two in the morning. She has to be at work by seven. What is this that has entered her life?

The man watches her. It feels as if he's saying something that's coming through the crown of her head. She clears away the cups, rinses them, and turns them down in the drain. Her hands are shaking. She folds her arms. She has all this pent up energy; she feels like a large cat wanting to spring. She cries quietly at first then begins to wail. Then she stops. Out the window, there is a pale light creeping over the horizon. She lights a wad of white cedar sage and walks through the house with it muttering the 23rd Psalm under her breath. When she is done, she feels clean, she feels light and emptied.

There is a knock on the door again. She drops her cup; it shatters on the floor. A voice. It's her neighbor, Bill.

Justine, are you all right, we heard you screaming?

Was she screaming? She opens the door. Charlene is with him. She is so relieved; she hugs them. Come in, come in, she says; she wants them to fill up the space with life, with sounds. She glances briefly outside the door before she shuts it. She thinks the boy is standing out there still. But that can't be. She returns to her friends.

Sit, sit, she tells them. I just had the strangest experience. There was this ringing and knocking on the door and when I opened it... She can't go any further. To utter it is to bring them back and to suffer again.

I am sorry, she says. She's been sitting on the green chair next to them. Now she is on her feet. Now she wishes them gone. She is ushering them out. I can't go into it. I have to put it behind me. I'm sorry. I know I must seem fragile.

Why don't we just stay with you for a while, Charlene says, standing up, drawing her close? You seem scattered.

I feel flustered, but thank you, I will explain again later.

They are out the door. She locks it again and fits the chain and leans back against it. She tries to catch her breath. She tries to think what to do. But the boy is beside her. She can only see him from the edges of her eyes. The head leaning to one side. But he is decidedly there. This time though she is strangely calm. She feels rooted. The boy takes her hand.

What do you want from me?

Love, he says quietly.

What!

He doesn't repeat himself. She's heard enough.

Where's the man?

Oh, he's gone; he just came to drop me off.

And who are you?

Paul, he says.

Is this a dream? Is this some horrible nightmare? She pinches herself.

I am tired, she blurts out. It's been a long night. And look, she says, peering at the horizon, morning is coming, a new dawn is breaking, isn't that great! She smiles at him. She is losing her mind. He is slowly breaking up; she doesn't see him as clearly or feel him as distinctly. Make yourself at home, she says, yawning. Might as well. You want love, she says. Well, we all want love. All we need is love, she is laughing and singing. Isn't life just great? she says. She is talking out loud in the room, she hears herself. Is this schizophrenia? she wonders briefly.

She turns off the light. She goes back down into her bedroom. She rolls into bed and covers herself. The boy sits on the chair facing the bed near the big eared croton. He watches her. She sees him there like a friend come to watch over her. She's not afraid. She's strangely comforted. She sleeps until late and when she wakes, he's gone.

She gets up to make tea and toast. It's Monday morning; she must head off to work soon. But the boy is there in the house; she can feel the buzzing in her chest. Strange. Her life now, this weird thing. She makes him Horlicks and they sit at the table.

She turns up the heat.

Who are you?

Paul, he says.

What do you want with me?

I've come to stay. I've been looking all over for you.

For me?

He nods. He slurps the mug.

Where are you from?

I'm a part of you. The part you dumped, the part you didn't want to have anything to do with.

She says nothing. This is crazy. She bites into crunchy toast; bits sprinkle about her plate.

How did you find me?

That man is a part of you too. He's just grown. He knows everything. He took me after you let me go.

She has to catch the bus in an hour. She wants to continue the conversation, but she doesn't want to. She wants him to clear the hell out.

I'm not leaving again, he says. I'm home now.

She has a date at seven with the man she's been seeing. She'll meet him for dinner; they'll go back to his apartment and fuck. Maybe she'll come home. Maybe she'll stay. She'll put extra clothes in her car.

She doesn't exactly know what to do with this predicament. From the corners of her eyes she watches, her gaze off focus. He dips his bread into the mug, he takes it into his mouth warm and soggy; he has a white rim of Horlicks above his lips. His eyes are still, chocolaty and still. She thinks she recognizes him, old family photos, but she is not sure. Why is she even contemplating this?

I've to get dressed for work. She pushes back her chair and heads downstairs. She showers quickly, blows her hair, her closet is neat, her shoes on the carpeted floor arranged by color and style. Her neighbors on the other side, their children are loud as they get ready for school. Their dogs are always barking. The woman is always shouting.

She says nothing to the boy, but he trots beside her as she lets herself out of the door and locks it. On the highway, there's bumper-to-bumper traffic. She turns the radio to NPR; he turns it off.

Talk to me, he says.

The rage swells up her face.

She turns it back on.

He dumps the whole radio out the window.

I am not afraid of you, she tells him through her teeth.

I've come all this way to find you, he says.

You are not wanted here. How much clearer, how much clearer do I need to be!

He says nothing. He looks out the window; he starts to sing under his breath – glory, glory, hallelujah, glory, glory hallelujah, glory, glory hallelujah, they crucified my lord.

Despite herself, her chest is welling up. Who are you, she cries.

He doesn't say anything. He sings his terrible song about glory.

Something is coming back to her, some memory, but it constantly eludes her; she only remembers the color brown. What's clear though is she'll have to use some other tack with him. You claim you're a part of me, she says, that I dumped you a long time ago. Then why are you back? I don't want you. Another thought is breaking in – what you resist, persists. But I didn't even resist anything. She is talking to herself now. I mean, Jesus Christ! And she slams her hands on the wheel.

I'm not leaving, the boy says again.

Why would anything, anyone return if they are not wanted?

I want to be whole, the boy says, and in the end, everything you've discarded, will, must find its way home for completion.

She parks, waits seven minutes for the shuttle, which will take her to campus where she teaches three classes of accounting back to back, Mondays, Wednesdays, and Thursdays. She's been teaching here for four years; that's where she met the man who is her lover; he is an administrator at the college.

But some people close themselves off forever, she says.

Not forever, he says, never forever. It's true we live a long, long time, many, many lifetimes, but eventually the discarded parts come home.

I don't like that term discarded, she says. They're walking now into the classroom.

If the hat fits, he says.

She looks at his face full of sass. He's smiling. She's smiling too.

Her class as usual is packed with students – so satisfying, she thinks, walking towards her desk.

She watches him from the corners of her eyes all day. He sits through three sets of accounting. Sometimes he dozes off, or she sees him climbing in and out the tall windows, somersaulting in the middle of the room; she watches him crawling along the ceiling, screwing and unscrewing the light bulbs. He is squirreling through her bangs; she flicks him out of her hair. He wants to know her. He's happy he's home.

She drives to see the lover. She picks up a roasted chicken from the store, a rocket salad, and a baguette. She wants to be home alone with him. She wants it different now somehow. She wants to tell him about the boy. She wants to show him the boy. Despite herself, despite herself.

I don't remember when you left, she says as they are driving. I don't remember you at all. And I am sorry, I mean, I have a good memory.

You couldn't help yourself, the boy says. You were a wreck.

This stings. A wreck.

It was after your father molested you.

She almost ploughs the car into the back of a truck. Where did you get that? She is almost screaming. Not almost, she is. She wants to heave him out the car. My father, she spits, God rest his soul, my father has never!

That's what I mean, he says quietly. Everything went, even the memory.

This is not fair. She starts to sob.

The boy is glued to the door, his eyes far, far away.

She wants him to leave.

I've already told you, the boy shouts. I am not leaving again. I am here now. Deal with me. It's a plea.

She pulls off the highway, eases her car over to a quiet side street. Her head is shrieking.

Papa, she says, and she is moaning and moaning. Papa.

Her father appears. Her jaw falls. Her father is tall and slim. He's wearing a brown suit and a molten blue tie. Her father used to be an accountant; he gave her his love of figures. I'm sorry, he says, his eyes are lowered, his head, his body, one big apology. I'm sorry.

She wants to be disgusted with the whole thing. But I don't remember, she says, I mean.

He takes her hand. It feels like butter. I didn't know better. Perhaps it's best not to remember. But know that I'm sorry, I'm truly sorry.

He leaves just as suddenly as he arrives. And the car is eerily still. She doesn't know what to do with her eyes, her heart that is searing her chest, her hands that want to crush something, the boy.

There is a man running with his dog. He runs towards them and nods as he passes. The dog's gaze wanders over and locks eyes with the boy. It slows. Come on buddy, the man whispers, and the dog picks up the pace again.

She digs furiously in her bag for Kleenex. She finds some and daubs at her face, blows her nose. Her mascara is a mess. Her entire face is a mess. The boy glued to the door has his face turned to the road. She says nothing to him. She has nothing else to say. She wants to be in the lover's arm, she wants to be tucked away, snuggled away. The world, she thinks in that moment, is a terrible place for little children, a terrible place. What will she say to this man, her lover, tonight?

The smell of the chicken fills up the car. She is famished. She tears off the plastic cover and pulls off a leg; she hands a wing to the boy and a napkin. He crumples the whole thing in his mouth; she watches the juice fall down his lips. She hears him crunching the bones under his powerful jaws; she turns away. She suddenly has no appetite whatsoever. She hands the boy the other leg. He stuffs the entire thing in his mouth, distending his face. His gluttony frightens her. It's as if he's starving for her.

She noses the car back onto the highway. She doesn't know where she wants to go, what she wants to do. This news is killing her. It's cutting off her breath, it's shrieking in her head, it's muddying her vision. Her father. Her poor, sweet father. She drives in the slow lane; her hands on the steering tremble slightly. The lover's exit is coming up, and if she passes it, she'll take the turn on another highway and twenty minutes later she'll be home. She doesn't know yet.

She texts the man, her lover, to let him know she'll meet him at his house. She pulls up abruptly at the curb. He is just backing out of the garage. I have food, she yells through the window, and then she remembers the disemboweled chicken. Never mind, she says. Let's just talk.

She sees the weariness come over his face like a shadow. She sees the falling down moustache. She swallows. She didn't even put her face back together. It's tear-streaked; it's puffy. The boy is looking at the ceiling of the car and scowling.

Leave him, he says, he's no good.

She sucks her teeth. And you are good. You've come back and you've brought only shit.

Leave him, now, he roars.

She goes quiet.

The man, the lover, is at the window. He's impatient. She can tell she's ruining his evening, messing up things.

He flicks a speck off his white shirt. What's happening? What's been going on? You've been crying?

Long day, she says quietly.

Should we go inside, get you a drink.

No. I mean, yes. Okay. She glances quickly at the boy and opens the door.

You've been crying?

It's nothing, she says, I just have to wash my face.

She follows him into the house. He brings her water after she's returned from the bathroom.

Why didn't you call? Should I order in?

So many questions. The boy has followed them in. He's wandering through the house, looking at this, fingering that. This man, her lover, collects marbles. He has teams of them out in glass bowls and saucers through the living room. Some of them cost thousands. The place is like a museum. The boy pockets one and the other he sends crashing through the window.

What the hell! The man had been sitting next to her; he had started to undo the buttons of her shirt. He leaps up at once. What is going on? His erection shrinks. He runs over to the window. There is a hole in the window, the size of a coin. He looks at her. He looks directly at the boy. Another marble pierces the glass window and he has several more in his hands poised to throw.

I should go, she says buttoning her shirt. This is too weird. I'm going, she says and slips out. She races to her car. She doesn't look again at the boy, she doesn't think, her heart is galloping in her chest; she races down the highway and puts the car in the garage.

In the house, she runs a bath and lowers herself into the boiling water. She wants to scream.

He appears in the doorway. He begins to hum a song. The melody of it takes her down slowly until she is able to find herself again. She breathes deeply and sweet.

He doesn't love you, the boy says.

You're the one who doesn't love me, she says, crying.

I wouldn't have come back then, he says. You would've just been here incomplete and rotting.

It's been havoc since you've returned.

You need to make room for me.

You can't come here and stir up things and impose. Who the fuck do you think you are?

He lights her a candle and leaves her there in the tub. I am you, he says. And I'm happy to be home.

She needs to talk to someone. It's like a prison, her life. That's what it's become since she opened that door.

The man, her lover, is calling on the phone. She doesn't pick up; it goes to voice mail. He's calling again. She picks up.

What the hell is going on? You ran out of here.

It was too weird, she says.

What are you doing, it's our time.

There's a lot going on.

When can I see you? You want me to come there?

He's never been to her house. There's desperation in his voice. She's never heard it before. I think we should stop, she says.

He's quiet. Really.

I need some time.

Time for what?

There's a lot going on.

Like what? Talk to me. Tell me.

How can she tell him about the boy and about her father and about her life now turned upside down?

My father molested me, she says.

She hears him sigh. She thinks he might be crying.

What a fucking bastard. You just found out, he says, you just remembered? Oh, God. I'm so sorry.

...

Let me come over. Let me comfort you.

...

Let me take care of you.

This is what she wants more than anything. The longing is excruciating. It takes over every cell in her body.

You deserve it, he is saying. After what that monster has done. Come, he says.

Her heart is breaking.

The boy appears in the doorway.

Why, she rages at him. Why can't I go to him?

He can't protect you.

I don't need protection. It's over now. He's dead. He's dead.

The lover is still on the phone. Hello, that you, hello.

She unplugs the phone, heaves herself out of the tub, splashing water all over the rug and the floor. You cannot come in here and rule my life. She is in a rage. She doesn't recognize her voice. You are a fraud. A damn fraud! She goes after him with the broom she uses to bang on the ceiling when her neighbors are screwing each other. I will kill you, she roars. You have hijacked my life. She breaks the broom into splinters on the wood floor. The boy is nowhere to be seen. She dresses. I'm going to have the man I choose. I am going to live my life. You go to hell!

She tears out the house and slams the door behind her. It's dusk. She walks into the hills past the palatial homes towering on the ridge. Lights soar in the windows. Dogs are barking, the sprinklers are hissing, birds are flying south. Kids are playing in their yards. She hears the dull layers of conversations. She needs a tree, any tree, and when she finds one, big and broad shouldered and secluded, she leans against it and wails.

The boy is beside her, the two of them sitting at the root of the tree. The boy is stroking her hair. He is humming a soft song. He is holding her face. Why didn't you protect me, he says. Why didn't you save me?

I couldn't. I didn't even know. I don't remember. Shit. If I'd known… She holds him close. If I'd known what to do, you'd be the first one. The boy is sobbing. Shit, I didn't know. I probably just wanted to disappear. I probably just said—this is what you want, okay, have it—and then I left my body and took myself elsewhere.

I'm the one you left there with him, the boy says. I'm the thing. The body.

She looks at him as if just seeing him. What do you mean?

Then she doesn't say anything else.

Night has arrived finally. The stars are out, the sky is full of them, and the forest is alive with all the creatures of the dark. She gets up. She follows the boy slowly home. They climb into bed together, they settle down into the wad of unmade sheets. She doesn't say anything to him or he to her. They don't touch. There is an oasis between them and a fertile line as well.

Where were you all this time?

The man took me. There were others of us. We knew we'd come back eventually, but we had to wait until you were ready.

What if I wasn't?

Eventually you'd be. Eventually you'd want all your selves back.

She isn't exactly a simple woman. There's a lot she knows about the world, but this is strange to her. Seeing imaginary figures is stranger. Though he isn't exactly imaginary, as she can see him, but then only she can. Does that make him real? Does that make her crazy?

And the place where you lived?

Oh, it's okay. It's like this. We're treated well. It's just that we're waiting to come back. We can see you. We're always hoping for the right time. We're waiting for a glimpse of an opening.

I didn't even know you were gone.

...

I mean, it's weird. She tapers off. I mean how can something so big, so monstrous happen and... I mean where does the memory go?

I have it, the boy says. I hold it right here. I am it.

But I don't want to remember it.

I know, the boy says. That's why I have it. And I have other things too. I have your whole life.

She laughs awkwardly. You're giving yourself a lot of credit.

It's a paradox. You can cut out the memory that is me, and you can cut out other things as well. To take me back is to take back your memories as well as your life.

I don't want those memories.

That is the paradox. You chopped off the hand but the fingers are useful too.

Too many riddles, she says. Furthermore you've come, and I have no space. You're killing my relationship.

How can the relationship be any good if I'm not part of it, part of you, if I'm not integrated?

Give me a break! She is getting angry again. Look, she says, you're pissing me off. Next thing you'll tell me you're holding parts of me from other lifetimes.

He chuckles. I am.

Please!

The sooner you accept me, the sooner we can integrate, the better your life will be.

Just like a man to say that! You are the center of the world, right?

You are the center. I am a part of you.

She jumps out of bed and heads to the refrigerator where there is a bottle of old wine. She eats slowly the leftover chicken she'd bought earlier; she drinks glass after glass of the bitter red wine.

He takes the bottle away. It doesn't have to be this way. Really.

How am I to accept you? I don't even remember. She is weeping now.

I am the memory. I am the split off part. If you stop fighting, if you stop resisting, maybe we can get somewhere.

I have to sleep, she says, turning away from him and crawling back into bed.

Okay, he says, he is sitting on the chair again near the speckled red croton facing her. I'll be here in the morning.

Oh God, she wails into the night. How did I deserve this shit?

When she wakes the man is sitting there. The man who'd come with the boy.

She jumps. Where is the boy?

He's here. He's just asked me to come. The split off parts of us only want to return for wholeness. They don't want separation. Everything is yearning for union.

I am not spiritual, she says. I don't understand this stuff. It's gibberish to me. You should take him back. It's a mistake. His coming here is a mistake.

You summoned him.

DID NOT! I don't remember him or when he left. He says my father did a horrible thing to me. I don't remember any of this. But then my father comes crying. The boy comes into my life and demands changes. Who does he think he is? And then I must jump to his wishes.

You are afraid and trusting is hard.

I wish you wouldn't analyze me. My life was fine, do you hear me, my life was fine before you came and now it's hell, hell, hell!

The man watches her; very gently he holds her with his eyes.

Do you want to remember, he says.

No!

Why?

I love my dad.

That wouldn't stop. Your dad loves you too. The loving, the healthy loving never stops.

Then why would he do that?

Darkness walks in all of us.

And you, aren't you in the dark?

No, he says, we're the part of you that is light, that wants the wholeness.

What then, if I remember?

You'll see how the splitting occurs.

What about the pain?

We'll show you how to work with that.

Why not just take it away altogether.

Not my job to do that.

I don't understand, she says.

Would you like to see it then?

No, she says.

We have time, he says.

She thinks it might have been a dream. She wakes refreshed. She heads off to school with the boy in the car. She says nothing to him. She meets her friends for lunch. She is not exactly angry with the boy; he is like a sixth finger. Perhaps she can ignore him or not let him get into her skin as much. He is there, always in the background, observing. She wants to meet her lover tonight. But she is a little queasy about that now. What if the boy starts acting the damn fool again? Her life is starting to feel like it's her own again. After work, she shops with her friends at the mall. She buys a new purse for herself, and for the boy, a kite with a dragon on it. She tells her friends it's for her nephew.

She meets her lover at the restaurant near his house. He's happy to see her. There's concern in his eyes. He kisses her, holds her close, holds her like some delicate, some precious thing. He fusses over her at dinner, and that night in his bed, he's gentle with her, he talks to her, he watches her eyes and her face. He holds her body to receive him. He's never this attentive. And the boy too is quiet. At one point he comes into the room. She doesn't meet his eyes, isn't interested in his accusations. He closes the door behind him and she waits, expecting him to smash a bottle or a glass, to start up with the marbles again, but nothing.

She sleeps pressed up to the man who it feels like she is noticing for the first time, his massive shoulders, his small belly, his thin hairy arm, his long fingers and toes. For hours after she feels his imprint inside her, feels the weight of him on her bones, feels his breath on her neck, his sweat soaked into her skin.

Are you ready now? he asks.

It's the man again, the man who accompanied the boy. I don't know, she says. In truth her resolve is breaking. She is feeling good now about life. She feels closer to her lover, now more than ever. The boy doesn't affect her as much. He is there. But sometimes it's as if he's not. Days go by and she forgets. But then, there he is again. They hardly speak now, if ever. She isn't ignoring him exactly, but he also doesn't make any more demands. He sleeps with her now at night, he on his side of the bed, she on hers. But that is it. There isn't animosity; perhaps that's integration of some sort, though she thinks not. They're just waiting, she thinks—in a holding pattern.

I am happy, she says, what is the point. Why bring sadness now. Why bring problems. Things are good.

It is as you wish, he says. You have your free will. I am here. Just call me.

And your name again?

Just think of me, he says. Your thoughts will call me.

She returns to her life. She feels no pressure. The boy is still there, but the boy she can live with. She means to tell the lover about him, but every time she tries, it's as if the boy is there, saying, NO; this is private. Still, she can live with that.

She wants to ask her mother about her father. Did her mother know? Is that why she eventually left the father and remarried? Her mother has always said, your father is not a good man, but she had seen him as glory. Her stepfather was good enough, but it was her father she adored. And then he was dead.

But now she wants to know. What if she integrates the boy, how would that change things? And why is it a boy, for crying out loud, and not a girl!

She calls him in again with her thoughts. Ok, she says, I'm ready. She's nervous as hell. She's alone in her room. She's asked the boy to leave.

The man sits with her. He has a kind round face. He takes her hands. He tells her to keep her eyes on him and move her consciousness to the center of her heart.

I can't do both, she says. She is trembling, but his hands on her are calming. And his eyes steady hers.

He starts to sing a song. Oh, how I love you. She feels like rolling her eyes. What is it with these two and the confounded singing! He doesn't sing loud. She doesn't know the song. Halfway through the second line, she is weeping. She doesn't know why. Her heart wants to burst. He is all over her, everywhere at once with something, something that feels like light, like feathers, and at the same time he is there with her singing his song and the room feels full of forms. She is sobbing and sobbing. He's singing her a song. Her heart. He holds her. You are love, he says over and over. The boy is there, the boy too is sobbing. What the hell is this, she is thinking through her tears. It's as if a hardened crust of her heart is being removed, is being pried off. She shrieks. And he says yes, yes, yes, you are love. And the entire thing last three minutes, maybe less, but it feels like a long, long time.

Rest now, rest. We are here with you. Rest now. And it does feel like there are people there around her bed, holding her, holding vigil for her heart. It's interesting, is all she can think to say. She sleeps.

She hasn't called her mother in months. She calls her mother.

It's been ages, her mother hoots.

Tell me about my dad, she says.

Not this again.

I know you said he wasn't a good man.

The mother is quiet on the phone. Why, she asks, why are you asking me this?

I don't know. Some stuff's been happening and I'm just wondering. Why didn't you tell me?

You don't tell children those things unless there are symptoms, you know, signs. You seemed okay. You seemed adjusted. I watched you for years.

She doesn't say anything else to her mother. What else can she say? Beside her the boy is curled up, his eyes closed, his breath even and deep, though she knows he's only pretending, his ears are cocked; he's been listening. What to say to her mother now but thank you. Maybe one day she'll tell her about the boy. I'll call again soon, she says into the phone. I must go now.

Everything is alright, the mother wants to know.

Yes, she says, touching the boy's face slightly. Everything is alright.

adrienne maree

enclaves

(written at the first detroit sci fi collective writing salon, mar 25, 2014)

detroit 2414

mlara was so so tired.

every time she walked out of her house it was a suffering. today she had left the house as herself but by the time she'd reached the central detroit grocer her hands were wisened and gnarled, and she could feel the skin hanging, used, from her face. she looked all of her 327 years. and no one looked their age anymore.

no one listened to the old, so she was ignored by everyone who came across her, barely tolerated by those who billed her for her rations.

it was risky enough, crossing the short wild blocks between her home and the grocer. being perceived as old was just an added danger.

going to get food meant leaving the safety of her neighbors and the rules their great grandparents had come up with for their four block radius, which was surrounded by low walls of rock and, in this season, snow, the walls that indicated that there was a people here, a people who had created a way of being with each other and if you didn't know that way, you'd be better off not to enter.

theirs wasn't one of the fancy enclaves. their robot was at least 500 years old now, and the enclave looked like it had been around at least that long. lately it was the worst she'd ever seen it. the bot could barely hold a steady projection of a pleasing natural world on their outer rim, much less design interior experiences of luxury.

she'd grown up in a dome of blue sky, wind blowing fields of wheat and corn around their farmhouses, right here. she'd hated leaving the enclave when she was younger. now the fields shuddered and flickered, and the color was off so that everything felt kind of gloomy.

mlara had slipped through some of the nicer enclaves when she used to be in charge of her shapeshifting. she knew that in some of them the robots created heated pools that dropped over vast cliffs, with views of mountains or even other galaxies, with homes that seemed to float in the air, filled with plush retrofiber carpeting and the latest organic synthetic tools and toys, some even generating food for the residents.

not so here. yes, they cared for each other, they had a mesh network in place to stay in touch with each other and were all connected by a virtual alarm system so they'd know if any of their number were harmed. but that was about as far as their technology could go on a good day.

the most valuable thing in this enclave, by far, was the garden, which bloomed 10 months of the year. it was a secret, of course, housed in the interior of a true stone storage warehouse that had lost its roof ages ago to fire. mlara's late mother had claimed to be the one who'd realized that enough sun landed inside to nourish plants.

mlara's neighbor and long ago lover susteen had created a system of glass and nutrient mirrors that helped the light reach every corner of the garden. they all worked the garden, and each week everyone within the walls had rights to all the produce they could carry in two hands, harvested in the darkness.

these days mlara never knew which skin would show up on her

body when, and thus when her neighbors would recognize her, when she'd be allowed to gather vegetables from the garden. she could no longer risk going to get her portion and knew it wouldn't be long before concerned neighbors came looking to see why she wasn't claiming her food or covering her shifts to guard the food.

what could she tell them?

she didn't understand why this was happening to her. for decades now she had been able to become whatever she needed to be in order to traverse this city. her enclave was almost all shapeshifters; in the early years they'd stuck together for safety and now it just made things easier. shapeshifters were really the only ones who could move between communities with any ease. in all the unofficial ways of the world, that was their job. they were the unseen translators, many of them working together to try to recreate a sense of unity across the vast geography of detroit.

but in order to officially be part of the unofficial shapeshifters, you had to show up for 'all meetings and assignments in your origin form.'

mlara was no longer able to reliably hold her origin form, particularly when she left the enclave. she'd tried to attend one meeting once her shifting went chaotic, but was turned away at the door by the evening's host, who vehemently defended their knowledge of exactly who the real mlara was, rejecting this imposter.

she didn't know how she could go on. she had to sneak in and out of her own community, was estranged from her work. and forget love—no one wanted to look at an intermittent old lady who had neither the power nor the resources to keep herself young. if she couldn't stay young she was going to die, from aging or from the dangers of being viewed as old in a city with no place for those who could not labor.

she felt so alone.

she began to drop down and the floor rose up to meet her, matching the somber nature of her shape and energy. she felt tears come to her eyes. when she went to wipe them away she found her hands now smooth and small, her child hands.

at least this is accurate, she thought. i am crying like a baby.

the knock on the door didn't immediately get her attention, so caught up was she in the full body act of weeping. it wasn't until the sound escalated to the level of someone kicking aluminum with steel toed boots that she really heard it. she ran to the entrance and was about to open it when she remembered to check herself in the mirror.

thank god—her origin form. deep brown eyes in smooth brown skin, golden hair rising from her head in fro shock, eyebrows naturally arched for sarcasm, her own full gorgeous mouth. She smiled just a little to see herself, and opened the door.

there was a circle of five women standing there. they were old women. they looked repulsive to her. she was glad that in this moment she didn't look like that.

'mlara?'

ew! how did they know her name?

'mlara you daft vain child. it's me, susteen!'

susteen?

she and susteen had been lovers in their twenties, had known every soft inch of each other ages and ages ago. they had worked the garden side by side, and had many adventures as shapeshifters moving across the interenclave wilderness of detroit. she'd been the main one to sit with susteen when her husbands died in an explosion at the shuttle factory, and when her daughter left the enclave to marry into the belle isle enclave, a closed community.

mlara had never seen her look like this.
'susteen? what happened to you? why are you so old?'

susteen cocked an aged eyebrow at her. mlara took a moment in shock to look more closely at the other women in the circle. slowly she recognized shandow, keysla, robin, and dayda before her. ancient, all.

'yes, yes see us now? we're all old. just like you.'

'oh, not me, i' mlara started, the lie coming without any intention in it. but the women gently, immediately started laughing in her face. she panicked and looked down at her hands. wrinkled again, covered in age spots. her shoulders dropped in defeat.

'yes, you, mlara. silly old girl. look this is happening to all of us, all of us in the enclave. we're pretty sure our bot is breaking down.' susteen led the uninvited women past mlara, into the house. they lowered their bodies onto furniture with care.

'it isn't just us. nothing,' dayda gestured at the map of detroit enclaves on mlara's resting screen, 'nothing is as it seems, mlara. we look our age, and the enclave looks like shit but so do the other enclaves! it's all a goddamn facade that the bots have been manifesting for us.'

'of course the bots manifest it for us, isn't that what they were created for?' mlara tucked her hands under her thighs, fidgeting to have these women seeing her this way. she felt ashamed, naked.

'it's a subtle thing, mlara. i am going to try to lift up for you a subtle difference ok?' susteen took on her most condescending tone and a few of the women snickered, though there was no real cruelty in it. mlara was trying to catch her reflection in the metal cabinet where she kept her journals, but stopped when the room got quiet.

'we thought the bots were making our enclaves,' this from keysla.

'but actually each bot is... fused to our minds somehow. creating an illusion for us.'

'and we're out of it!' susteen burst in. 'i know this sounds cheesy, but it feels like freedom once you believe it!'

mlara looked around at them, at her home, trying to understand.

'why should all this affect my capacity to shapeshift, though?'

'you have no capacity to shift, honey. none of us do. it was one of the symbiotic emergent benefits of some of the bots. but now those bots are so out of date there aren't any parts left to try and fix it up.' keysla looked sad.

'i'm not a shapeshifter?'

susteen and the other women shook their heads. shandow spoke: 'don't appear to be. us neither. that was just our enclave's... story. what our bot made feel real in our minds. we are still trying to understand the ways bots communicate to each other about the illusions between enclaves, but... yeah, no shifters.'

mlara's body felt wild. she couldn't believe this—she knew what it felt like in her bones to shift. 'but how did the bots make it feel like that?'
susteen looked frustrated. 'it doesn't matter, because the bots are dying. and we are suddenly alive, maybe for the first time. we are real. free.'

'free to be old?' mlara spat out the words, voice rising. pointing to her face. 'to die?'

'we've been old, mlara. for some time now,' susteen said, tired voice, tired shrugging shoulders.

'the older bots like ours, they just can't maintain the illusions anymore.' keysla's voice was low, weaving this information in.

mlara looked around at them, familiar, stranger. they had each been such gorgeous young women for so long now.

mlara felt the shock through her system. how could this be? she looked at her hands, which felt suddenly small and temporary. she wondered if she should just give up now, just fall over and die.

'mlara.' susteen was close to her now, grabbing her hand. 'mlara girl come now. are you listening to me? we might be the only ones who still remember how to grow food the old way. we can survive, maybe teach others. to our knowledge, no other enclave has maintained a garden.'

'or every enclave has maintained a secret one,' mlara replied in a dazed monotone with only a small inflection of sarcasm.

'or that. there is no evidence at all of that. but it is possible.' shandow flipped her hands back and forth as she spoke, always fair.
'it's possible. unlikely. but for right now, we are in a perfect position. we have food. we have each other. we have no illusions, nothing is being done for us. and it is incredible. we are free to have a real life. not all of this miserable projection and extension. a real life. a life that ends.'

mlara stood up and walked to the mirrorwall. she watched now as her face shifted before her eyes. origin form, then briefly child, blond hair shifting from the root above her cocoa skin. And then all of it resolving into her very old, natural face, skin soft, translucent as a roasted garlic peel.

'we can feed everyone within our walls. that isn't an illusion.' keysla said this with a small smile in her voice.

'and you know, how those little walls around our home make it possible for us to have abundance inside.' shandow's voice was nearly a whisper. 'death is like that too, perhaps. a boundary that allows for something real to happen inside the time we have left.'

mlara felt the tears come into her face and then felt again the shame of being seen as she was. it was such an utterly unfamiliar feeling.

susteen came up behind her and placed arthritic hands on her shrinking shoulders. she leaned her pursed lips in and kissed mlara's neck, pulling mlara back into her soft body. mlara looked up and saw herself again.

she was an old woman, her hair white and soft and still standing up straight above her head. holding her was a dark skinned black woman with gray braids, her eyes full of tenderness and energy. in the reflection she saw the circle of brown soft elders.

they all looked released.

she had been making her life longer and then surviving it for so long. she felt the exhaustion flow through her. she didn't have to sneak around anymore, she didn't have to be alone. for the first time she could remember, all she had to do was be here.

Kay Ulanday Barrett

Brown Out Shouts!

this is for Matea who dances the bomba
with hands that crest moonhips
and who admittedly kisses harder
than she loves herself.

every trans, genderqueer, futchie, fairy, AG, butch queen,
anything with roots arches toward her, their arms like petals
soaking up her light.

and this is for hard ass Krys who doesn't want anything
to do with brasso or that jrotc uniform, but just
wants 3 meals a day for his brother
and a brand new binder for his chest.

for Javi, who takes his tequila quick.

for **Aqua Starr Black**.
because they had the bravery to re-name
themselves: aqua. starr. black.
sometimes you just gotta call out your power
cuz no one else is gonna do it for you.

Maria is a dancer clasping onto hardwood by the heels
but serves our coffee at the diner always wit' a smile
and always with her hair on-point
she's pissed off cuz her wife cannot afford to go to the hospital.
although, you can't see it, her heart breaks because no papers

or government can explain how this person in the bed makes her
laugh like a guttural fool.

for JP who draws sketches sneaking them in your purse.

for Celiany whose caliber demands that the very least of her lovers
(and play partners) have the following traits:
		dexterity, initiative, and someone who can "lay it down."

for every son shaped in bullets, your heart as compact as
a trigger, your voice a sharp wind song that wants to lay a forehead
down on the chest of your boyfriend.
let your letters survive the wars, jail cells,
let the meter of your words swoon your lover back to the bed,
as you take turns turning off the alarm on the nightstand with
your toes,	elbows,	orgasms,	and	in between kisses.

for that lonely Korean guy Jake who found me in a group of
500 white people in the frenzy of the Sugar Club in Dublin, Ireland.
		I make due, he said.

		We've got one grocery store and I practically live there.
		I mean, my kimchi is decent.

We can still see him shrugging
in the strobe lights, hungry for somewhere else.

this is for you this afternoon, spring cleaning your blues away,
maybe in your favorite t-shirt, maybe you called in sick,
maybe your body rattles, maybe missing your pamilya back home,
maybe you are waiting for that next shot to find home in yourself,

maybe your voice is hoarse from asking strangers for food,
maybe you lost a loved one or are about to loose yourself,
lost in the whimsy of musical notes.
the rhythms can consume the sadness, if you let it.

for my dearest Sarwat who sat on a hill, held up the sun, looking at all the fiiiine transgender and queers of color and said without saying,

> *Umm. I am not going that plenary/workshop/speech. You go on ahead. I'm gonna stay here. mm hmmm, I deserve this.*

for español,
pangasinan,
patois,
pidgin,
mandarin
love poems you write.

for those babydykes
       and trans youth who sprout out from
              the neighborhoods described to tourists as,
                     don't go there. it's dangerous.
           rolling up their windows from our existence.

for you who fights for our rights,
for you who laughs too loud,
for you who eats too much,
for you who twists wrists by paintbrush,
for you who will not let your spirit pass up a sunset or a protest
even when you think you deserve less sometimes.

for **you**
because there's a brown out right now
and by that I mean there is no electricity,
which means life is crashing and pouring down

and by that I mean I am lonely,
which really means
that we are brown and trans and queer and out
and we've been told too many times that all of those
cannot belong all at once. that based on those odds,
we equal death.

for you / for us / for we
because without explanation, we exist
and you, you like all of our ancestors before,
you live it so fiercely that even when injustice sets in,

this rumbling sky houses your breath and
that is better than any survival story,
that, that is joy being born.

Amir Rabiyah

Our Dangerous Sweetness

When I hear the news,
another one of us has been killed
my heart constricts,
I reach with a frantic grief
towards a soothing balm, difficult to find
I can't help but think of all the times
my life has been threatened
of all the people I love, and their lives

I am tired of being afraid
to speak my name
to unbind my chest
to be feminine and masculine
to go outside

I am tired of being afraid
of being brown
I am tired of being afraid
of my own existence
of revealing my full self
for fear that if I do, I will be killed

Here: I am the living impossibility
like so many of the people I love
who have the audacity to embrace themselves

Each day,
I feel departed souls swirl surround me
I feel thousands of hands brushing away my tears

They say: do what you were born to do
To write these words down
To write myself into wholeness
To write myself away from vengeance
They say: listen and so I listen
For a long time, I listen

Then they say speak
to those that are still here
& so I speak,
to those of you still here
I speak to say:

My Dear Beautiful People,
Each time you are broken,
I break, I break,   I break a little more
then un-break,
I am piecing myself back together
with the care of a potter's hands
I clay phoenix

I feel the heat
of our resurrections burning
to glaze our skin into glow
my fire and my kiln
are these words, this space
the intimate threads
of our connection

my prayer: we remember
ourselves as entwined in this struggle
my prayer: we undo the knots
we have tied around ourselves
we breathe
we remember we can be bound together
& free

I write because I feel the pulse of us
chanting the names of those who have died
Our own names
Our essences as holy
I envision us going on
to eclipse, building, bigger, bigger, bigger
more luminous

So bright
My beautiful people
our breaking is our making
& if I strip all my other identities away:
I am simply a poet who listens

To God,
To the dead,
To the living,
To all left behind,
To all the places in between,

I am simply a poet
who writes these words because I believe in us
because I know a faith uncontainable by an alphabet

My beautiful people let us dream towards
what we want
beyond survival
Let us dream towards loving ourselves
till we become love over & over again
My beautiful people
I can taste our honeyed victory

My beautiful people
our dangerous sweetness
is our rebellion

We are
Writing the Walls Down

Alexis Gumbs

Alexis Pauline Gumbs is a queer black troublemaker, a black feminist love evangelist and an afro-antillean grandchild living in Durham, North Carolina. Alexis is the founder of the *Eternal Summer of the Black Feminist Mind:* an intergalactic community school and the co-founder of *The Mobile Homecoming Project:* an experiential archive amplifying generations of black LGBTQ brilliance. Alexis is the author of many scholarly articles and several collections of poetry including *Ogbe Oyeku: Black Feminist Book of the Dead and Unborn, 101 Things That Are Not True About the Most Famous Black Women Alive,* and *Good Hair Gone Forever.* "an element of radical waywardness" is an excerpt from her forthcoming book *Spill.*

alexispauline.com

Ahimsa Timoteo Bodhrán

Ahimsa Timoteo Bodhrán is the author of *Antes y después del Bronx: Lenapehoking* (New American Press) and editor of an international queer Indigenous issue of *Yellow Medicine Review: A Journal of Indigenous Literature, Art, and Thought.* His work appears in 175 publications in Africa, the Américas, Asia, Australia, Europe, and the Pacific, including *Gender Outlaws: The Next Generation, Inclined to Speak: An Anthology of Contemporary Arab American Poetry, I Was Indian: An Anthology of Native Literature,* and *Troubling the Line: Trans and Genderqueer Poetry and Poetics.* He is completing *Yerbabuena/Mala yerba, All My Roots Need Rain: mixed-blood poetry & prose.*

pw.org/content/ahimsa_timoteo_bodhrán

Vanessa Huang

Home in diaspora from Atlanta and Oakland to Taipei, Vanessa Huang is a poet, interdisciplinary artist, and cultural organizer who weaves poemsongs with moments of transformative encounter, in call and response with kindred spirits who dream and make worlds where each and all of us are free. A 2014 Pushcart nominee, Vanessa's poetry and practice inherit teachings from the prison abolition, migrant justice, gender liberation, transformative justice, disability justice, and reproductive justice movements.

vanessahuang.com

Gaza song pg. 15

Amal Rana

Amal Rana is a Jeddah born, Pakistani poet/arts educator and VONA/Voices and Banff Centre Spoken Word Residency alum. In a time when even exhaling while being Muslim seems to have become a crime, she sees poetry as an act of sedition and collective resistance. Her work features in numerous journals, anthologies, and online platforms including *Your Voice Tastes Like Home: Immigrant Women Write, Adrienne: A Journal for Queer Women, Samar South Asian Magazine for Action and Reflection,* and *The Feminist Wire.* Her monologue about her family's history of displacement and racial profiling has been performed in multiple cities, academic institutions, and community events. She continues to organize projects and events that prioritize the voices of emerging QTIPOC and mixed race artists.

rosewaterpoet.com

when the skies were free pg. 19

Amir Rabiyah

see editor bio pg. 253

Grand Design pg. 21
Your Body Burns In Your Room pg. 22
Our Dangerous Sweetness pg. 229

Andrea Lambert

Andrea Lambert is the author of *Jet Set Desolate* (Future Fiction London, 2009), *Lorazepam and the Valley of Skin* (valeveil, 2009), and the chapbook *G(u)lit* (Los Angelene, 2011). She has an MFA in Critical Studies from CalArts and a BA from Reed College. Her work has appeared in HTMLGIANT, 3:AM Magazine, Ready, Able, Queer Mental Health, *The LA Telephone Book*, Loved Lettered, *Chronometry*, and *Off the Rocks #16*.

andreaklambert.com

Invocation pg. 23

Margaret Robinson

Dr. Margaret Robinson is a Mi'kmaw scholar and bisexual activist based in Toronto. She holds a PhD from the University of St. Michael's College. Margaret is currently a researcher in residence in Indigenous Health at the Ontario HIV Treatment Network and is an affiliate scientist with the Centre for Addiction and Mental Health. Margaret is passionate about intersectionality, postcolonial theory, and Aboriginal self-government.

Standing in the Intersection: Aboriginality, Sexuality and Mental Health pg. 29

Eli Clare

White, disabled, and genderqueer, Eli Clare happily lives in the Green Mountains of Vermont where he writes and proudly claims a penchant for rabble-rousing. He has written a book of essays *Exile and Pride: Disability, Queerness, and Liberation,* and a collection of poetry *The Marrow's Telling: Words in Motion,* and has been published in many periodicals and anthologies. He is currently finishing a book about cure called *Brilliant Imperfection: Grappling with Cure.* Eli speaks, teaches, and facilitates all over the United States and Canada at conferences, community events, and colleges about disability, queer and trans identities, and social jus-

(Eli Clare cont.)

tice. Among other pursuits, he has walked across the United States for peace, coordinated a rape prevention program, and helped organize the first ever Queerness and Disability Conference.

eliclare.com

Might the Walls Begin Again pg. 38

Jordan Rice

Jordan Rice is the author of *Constellarium* (Orison Books, 2016) and co-editor of the anthology *Voices of Transgender Parents* (Transgress Press, 2015). Her poems have been selected for the *Indiana Review* Poetry Prize, the *Gulf Coast* Poetry Prize, the Yellowwood Poetry Prize from *Yalobusha Review*, the Richard Peterson Poetry Prize from *Crab Orchard Review*, the Milton-Kessler Memorial Prize from *Harpur Palate*, and an AWP Intro Journals Award. Her poems have also been anthologized in *Writing the Walls Down: A Convergence of LGBTQ Voices*, *Troubling the Line: Trans and Genderqueer Poetry and Poetics*, *The Southern Poetry Anthology: Volume V*, *Best New Poets 2011*, *A Face to Meet the Faces: An Anthology of Contemporary Persona Poetry*, *Best of the Web 2009*, and *Best New Poets 2008*. Rice received an M.F.A. from Virginia Commonwealth University and a Ph.D. from Western Michigan University, where she served as Associate Editor for New Issues Poetry & Prose and as Assistant Poetry Editor for *Third Coast*. She currently teaches at Durham Technical Community College and is Executive Editor for *Dublin Poetry Review*.

Tresses pg. 44
Birthright pg. 46

Alfonzo Moret

Alfonzo Moret is a media artist working in mixed media painting, writing, and art installation. He has lectured at UC Berkeley, San Francisco Art Institute, and College of Arts

(Alfonzo Moret cont.)

and Crafts. He has a M.F.A. in Video Art, Film History, and Mixed Media from the University of California San Diego. His last solo exhibit "Speaking in Tongues" was based on the converging of African spiritualism and Christian concepts, which manifested in the form of a Santeria house of worship. This exhibit clearly challenged the viewing public at Saddleback College in Orange County; when the exhibit moved to Mesa College in San Diego, it stimulated dialogue with the public regarding faith and cultural myths.

Moret was born in Los Angeles, California, and raised in Watts, California; his family lineage is a mixture of Native American, African, Spanish, and French. His father was a jazz musician from Louisiana, and his mother a Black Cherokee from Oklahoma. In 1999 his large-scale video installation "House of Veils" at the Los Angeles African American Museum, made the cover of the *LA Times* Arts section. Moret's video installation took the form of a small scale tarpaper shack; in the windows and door frame, we glimpse history seen in films that depict stereotypes and myths associated with African American history. He investigated this topic using film history and various African American poets' written words in subtitles below the moving image, to give voice to the silent images.

In 2011 Moret presented a collection of paintings in an exhibition at San Francisco State University, called "Memoirs of Shadows."

Daniel Chan
Daniel is an aspiring poet who lives in Singapore.

H. Melt

H. Melt is a poet and artist who was born in Chicago. Their work proudly documents Chicago's queer and trans communities. Their writing has been published by Chicago Artist Writers, Lambda Literary, and THEM, the first trans literary journal in the United States. They are the author of *SIRvival in the Second City: Transqueer Chicago Poems* and currently work at the Poetry Foundation as the Education and Youth Services Assistant.

hmeltchicago.com

Sororicide pg. 50

Jerrold Yam

Jerrold Yam (b. 1991) is a law undergraduate at University College London and the author of three poetry collections, *Intruder* (Ethos Books, 2014), *Scattered Vertebrae* (Math Paper Press, 2013), and *Chasing Curtained Suns* (Math Paper Press, 2012). His work has been featured in *Time Out Magazine*, *Prairie Schooner*, *Southeast Asia Globe*, *Third Coast*, *Wasafiri*, and *Washington Square Review*. He has received poetry prizes from the British Council, National University of Singapore, and Poetry Book Society, and has been featured at the Ledbury Poetry Festival (2014), London Book Fair (2013), and Singapore Writers Festival (2013, 2014). He is named by Singapore's National Arts Council as one of the "New Voices of Singapore 2014".

jerroldyam.com

Communion pg. 51
Psalm pg. 52
Police pg. 53
Invincible pg. 54
Gift pg. 55

Danez Smith

Danez Smith is the author of *[insert] boy* (YesYes Books, 2014) and a forthcoming collection from Graywolf Press. He is a member of the Dark Noise Collective.

(Danez Smith cont.)

librecht baker

librecht baker is a playwright, poet, a member of the Dembrebrah West African Drum and Dance Ensemble in Long Beach, CA, as well as a Voices of Our Nation Arts Foundation (VONA/Voices) alumnae. She has a MFA in Interdisciplinary Arts from Goddard College. Her poetry is also included in *CHORUS: A Literary Mixtape* (MTV Books 2012).

Helen Klonaris

- see editor bio pg. 253

TC Tolbert

TC Tolbert often identifies as a trans and genderqueer feminist, collaborator, dancer, and poet but really s/he's just a human in love with humans doing human things. The author of *Gephyromania* (Ahsahta Press 2014) and co-editor of *Troubling the Line: Trans and Genderqueer Poetry and Poetics* (Nightboat Books 2013), his favorite thing in the world is Compositional Improvisation (which is another way of saying being alive). Thanks to Movement Salon and the Architects, TC keeps showing up and paying attention. Gloria Anzaldúa said, *Voyager, there are no bridges, one builds them as one walks.* John Cage said, *it's lighter than you think.*

tctolbert.com

Alex Simões

Alex Simões was born in 1973, Salvador, Bahia, Brazil. He is a poet, writer, multiartist, and professor. His book of sonnets, *Quarenta e Uns Sonetos Catados*, was published in 2013. His project "{hai} ceufies," combining haikus and mobile pictures, appeared in a poetry fanzine in 2014. In addition, his work appears in several anthologies and poetry magazines in Brazil.

toobitornottoobit.blogspot.com.br

sobre morrer pg. 84
eu canto pras paredes pg. 88
Soneto À Ladeira Da Montanha pg. 90

Tiffany Higgins

Tiffany Higgins is author of *And Aeneas Stares into Her Helmet* (Carolina Wren Press, 2009), selected by Evie Shockley as winner of the Carolina Wren Poetry Prize. In August 2014, she was artist-in-residence at Art Farm in Nebraska. Her poems appear in *Poetry, The Kenyon Review, Massachusetts Review, Taos Journal of Poetry & Art, From the Fishouse*, and other journals. She writes on ecology's intersection with culture and translates emerging Brazilian poets. Originally from Massachusetts, she teaches at several colleges in the San Francisco Bay Area.

tifhiggins.blogspot.com

on dying pg. 86
i sing through walls pg. 89
Sonnet to the Ladeira of the Mountain pg. 91

Sônia Maria Chaves Nepomuceno

Sônia Maria Chaves Nepomuceno is a photographer from Bahia. She is Bachelor of Laws and teaches Physical Education and History.

photo: Soneto À Ladeira Da Montanha pg. 90

Fabian Romero

Fabian Romero is a Queer Indigenous writer, performance artist and activist. They co-founded and participated in several writing, and performance groups including *Hijas de Su Madre, Las Mamalogues,* and *Mixed Messages: Stories by People of Color.* Their sincere writing stems from their intersections of privileges and marginalizations. You can read their work in several zines and publications including their writing blog, *Troubling the Line: Trans and Genderqueer Poetry and Poetics,* and in *Queer and Trans Artists of Color: Stories of Some of our Lives.* Fabian was born in Michoacán, Mexico and came to North America when they were seven years old. Since 2007 they have performed and facilitated workshops throughout North America. They have a BA from Evergreen State College with a focus in writing, social justice, and education.

fabianromero.com

Drugs and Capitalism: How Sobriety is Part of My Resistance pg. 92

Celeste Chan

Celeste Chan is an experimental artist, writer, and organizer. A Hedgebrook, Lambda Literary, SF Writer's Grotto, and VONA fellow, her writing can be found in *Ada, As/us journal, Feminist Wire, Hyphen,* and *Matador.* Her films have screened in CAAMFest, Digital Desperados, Entzaubert, Frameline, Heels on Wheels, MIX NYC, and Vancouver Queer Film Festival, among others. She has presented and curated in the SF Bay Area, NYC, Seattle, Bloomington, Glasgow, Berlin, and beyond. Alongside KB Boyce, she co-directs Queer Rebels, a queer and trans people of color arts project.

celestechan.com
queerrebels.com

Still from the short film "Bloodlines" pg. 104

micha cárdenas

micha cárdenas is an artist, theorist, and educator who creates and studies trans of color movement in digital media, where movement includes migration, performance, and mobility. micha is a Provost Fellow and PhD candidate in Media Arts + Practice (iMAP) at University of Southern California and a member of the artist collective Electronic Disturbance Theater 2.0. micha's solo and collaborative work has been seen in museums, galleries, biennials, keynotes, community, and public spaces around the world. Her co-authored books *The Transreal: Political Aesthetics of Crossing Realities* and *Trans Desire / Affective Cyborgs* were published by Atropos Press. Her work has appeared in the anthologies *Troubling the Line, The &Now Awards 3, Gender Outlaws, Queer Geographies, The Critical Digital Studies Reader,* and the *Feminist and Queer Information Studies Reader,* as well as in *The Journal of Popular Music Studies,* the *Ada Journal of Gender, New Media and Technology,* and the *AI & Society Journal,* as well as the magazines *No More Potlucks, Mute Magazine,* and *make/shift magazine.*

michacardenas.org

Janine Mogannam

Janine Mogannam is a poet, librarian, and 2.5-generation San Franciscan, by way of Palestine. She is a VONA Voices workshop alumna and a winner of the Friends of the San Francisco Public Library's PoetsEleven poetry contest. Her work has been featured in *580 Split, Kweli Journal,* and *Dismantle: An Anthology of Writing from the VONA/Voices Writing Workshop.*

Indira Allegra

Indira Allegra is the winner of the Jackson Literary Award, recipient of the Oakland Individual Artist grant, and a former Lambda Literary Fellow; she has been interviewed by BBC Radio 4, *make/shift magazine* and artactivistnia.com. She has contributed works to *HYSTERIA Magazine, Writing Home: Award-Winning Literature from the New West, Yellow Medicine Review: A Journal of Indigenous Literature, Art and Thought*, and *Sovereign Erotics: A Collection of Two Spirit Literature* among others.

Allegra's short films have screened at festivals such as MIX NYC, Perlen Hannover LGBT Festival, Outfest Fusion, and Bologna Lesbian Film Festival. She has been actively involved in artist residencies and lectures at the University of Oregon, East Carolina University, and The Banff Centre in Canada. In the Bay Area, her group exhibitions include SOMArts, Oliver Art Center, and Alter Space galleries.

indiraallegra.com

Ahmunet Jessica Jordon

Ahmunet is a Black, queer poet, writer, and educator from Baltimore. She is committed to sharing raw stories of the Black experience to ignite change, transformation, and healing through art. Ahmunet's main focuses are punchy poetic prose narratives investigating the somatic experience of love, space, and spirituality. She received her MFA in Writing and Consciousness from The California Institute of Integral Studies in San Francisco.

ahmunet.com

Rajiv Mohabir

Winner of the 2014 Intro Prize in Poetry by Four Way Books, Rajiv Mohabir's *The Taxidermist's Cut* is forthcoming Spring 2016. He received fellowships from Voices of Our Nation's Artist foundation, Kundiman, and the American Institute of Indian Studies language program, and his poetry and translations have been published or are forthcoming from journals such as *Prairie Schooner, Crab Orchard Review, Drunken Boat, Asian American Literary Review,* and *diode.* He completed his MFA at Queens College where he was Editor in Chief of the *Ozone Park Literary Journal.* Rajiv Mohabir currently pursues a PhD from the University of Hawai`i.

rajivmohabir.com

Aaron M. Ambrose

Aaron Ambrose is a poet. A queer, white, scorpio femme. Sick, disabled, and welfare class. Born and raised in Rochester, New York, she's been drying out in New Mexico for 20 years. Currently studying to become a community herbalist, Aaron also happens to be a fabulous step-parent, craftsman, and resale queen.

poeticoverthrow.blogspot.com

Jennie Kermode

Jennie Kermode is an author and journalist who works as a commissioning editor at *Eye For Film* and chairs the charity Trans Media Watch.

jenniekermode.com

July Westhale

July Westhale is a Fulbright-nominated poet, activist, and journalist. She has been awarded residencies from the Vermont Studio Center, Lambda Literary Foundation, Sewanee, Napa Valley, Tin House, and Bread Loaf. Her poetry has most recently been published in *Adrienne, burntdistrict, Eleven Eleven, Sugar Mule, The East Bay Review, 580 Split, Quarterly West*, and *PRISM International*. She is the 2014 Tomales Bay Poetry Fellow.

julywesthale.com

lee boudakian

is a queer, gender diverse, Lebanese-Syrian-Armenian mixie living in Vancouver, unceded Coast Salish territories. they are cultivating a practice that includes interdisciplinary art-making, writing, performing, community organizing, and facilitating arts-based workshops. their work explores intersectional identities and social justice – seeking to share un(der)represented stories of survival and make visible systemic oppressions that impact daily life, relationships, and bodies.

deararmen.com

Heidi Andrea Restrepo Rhodes

Heidi Andrea Restrepo Rhodes is a queer, mixed-race, second-generation Colombian immigrant, writer, scholar, artist, and activist. She is committed to creative work as a practice of witness, social documentation, historical memory, of radical healing, of provocation to action, and as a tool for liberation. Her poetry has been seen or is forthcoming in a number of literary journals and anthologies, including *Kudzu House Review, As/Us, Feminist Studies Journal, Nepantla, Yellow Medicine Review, Write Bloody's 'We Will Be Shelter'* and others. She currently lives in Brooklyn.

Vivian Lopez

Vivian Lopez is a high school English teacher with an MFA in Literary Translation from CUNY Queens College. Her poem "To Speak of Ghosts" was published in *decomP! Magazine*; her translation of María Elena Cruz Varela's poem "Intimidad y Fuga"/"Privacy & Escape" was published in *Mead Magazine*; and her translations of Juan Antonio Bernier's poems "Tu Sonrisa"/"Your Smile," "Mediodía"/"Noon," and "El Invierno, de Nuevo"/"Winter Again" have been published in *Aldus, A Journal of Translation*.

El Otro Lado pg. 146

Trish Salah

Born in Halifax, Trish Salah is a writer, activist, and professor of Women's and Gender Studies at the University of Winnipeg. In 2014 she co-organized an international Trans Literature conference, Writing Trans Genres, and co-edited an issue of *TSQ: Transgender Studies Quarterly* on Cultural Production. She has writing in recent and forthcoming issues of *Atlantis, Tripwire, TSQ, Lemonhound, Recours au Poème*, and in the collections *The Electric Gurlesque, Trans Activism in Canada: A Reader, Selling Sex*, and *Troubling the Line*. She has two books, the Lambda Award-winning *Wanting in Arabic*, and *Lyric Sexology, Vol. 1*.

Offer the desert, the tower pg. 149
Poem for Abousfian Abdelrazik pg. 154

Nayrouz Abu Hatoum

Nayrouz Abu Hatoum is a PhD Student in Social Anthropology at York University. Nayrouz grew up in Palestine and moved to Toronto in 2004 to pursue her graduate education. She occasionally writes poetry in both English and Arabic, and often entertains herself with the exercise of translating poetry between Arabic and English.

dalaala.com

قدّم البرج للصّحراء pg. 151
إهداء لأبو سفيان عبد الرازق pg. 155

Minal Hajratwala

Minal's latest book is *Bountiful Instructions for Enlightenment*, published by The (Great) Indian Poetry Collective. She is a writing coach, author of the award-winning *Leaving India: My Family's Journey from Five Villages to Five Continents*, and editor of *Out! Stories from the New Queer India*.

minalhajratwala.com

Aiyyana Maracle

Aiyyana Maracle is an award-winning multi-disciplinary artist; a Haudenosaunee great-grandma.

Having recently moved back to her Rez, she is pondering some, playing some, enjoying the discovery of what sort of art and writing may emerge from this portion of her life's journey.

Vickie Vértiz

Vickie Vértiz was born and raised in southeast Los Angeles. Her writing can be found in the *Los Angeles Review of Books*, KCET Departures, *Statement*, *Ghost Town*, and the anthologies *Open the Door* (from McSweeney's and the Poetry Foundation) and *Orangelandia* (from Inlandia Press). Vickie teaches or has taught creative writing to adults and young people at places like 826 Valencia, Boyle Heights libraries, the Claremont Colleges, and at the University of California, Riverside. Her poetry collection *Swallows* was published in 2013 by Finishing Line Press. She is at work on a memoir about her education titled *Smart: Growing up Gifted and Brown in Southeast Los Angeles*.

vertiz.wordpress.com

Hannah J Stein

Hannah J Stein is from Athens, Georgia and graduated from Lawrence University in 2013. She is currently a theatrical production assistant for 20% Theatre Company in Minneapolis. She would like to thank her family, teachers, and friends for their support.

Polished Glass pg. 174

Dane Slutzky

Dane Slutzky is a Jewish, genderqueer writer who relies on poetry and science fiction as outlets for escapist rage. Dane lives in the southern Oregon rainforest where he learns about eco-forestry, natural building, and off-grid energy systems.

daneslutzky.com

Birthright pg. 180

Moon Flower

Moon Flower is a Native, two spirit tribal scholar and has been a Lecturer in American Indian Studies with a special focus in Literature and Media at San Francisco State University. Her poems and art have appeared in *Red Ink Magazine, Kweli Journal, Mujeres de Maiz (Women of Corn),* among others and the anthology *Other Tongues: Mixed-Race Women Speak Out.* She has shared the stage with Mystic, Quese IMC, Audiopharmacy, and many gifted performers. This past year she completed her first creative short film entitled *Ehecatl Wind Medicine.*

moonflower.biz

Arizona F/law pg. 181

Joy Ladin

Joy Ladin is the author of six books of poetry, including last year's *The Definition of Joy,* Lambda Literary Award finalist *Transmigration,* and Forward Fives award winner *Coming to Life;* her seventh collection, *Impersonation,* is due out in 2015. Her memoir, *Through the Door of Life,* was a 2012 Na tional Jewish Book Award finalist. Her work has appeared in many publications, including *American Poetry Review, Prairie Schooner, Parnassus: Poetry in Review, Southern Review, Southwest Review, Michigan Quarterly Review,* and *North American Review,* and has been recognized with a Fulbright Scholarship. She holds the David and Ruth Gottesman Chair in English at Stern College of Yeshiva University.

Thokozane Minah

Thokozane Minah is a 20 something queer, genderqueer artist and writer of Zulu, Swati, and Ndebele descent, living in South Africa and working towards qualifying as a high school educator. They have had their work published in *Queer Africa: New and Collected Fiction* as well as in various blogs such as the Bklyn Boihood Bois will be Bois, Black Girl Dangerous, and HOLAA (Hub of Loving Africa), as well as online magazine *Interrupt Mag.*

arevolutionaryboi.blogspot.com

deborah brandon

deborah brandon lives in Tucson and holds an MFA in Writing from the School of the Art Institute of Chicago. Additional work appears in *Transom, Ocho, MiPOesias, here/there: poetry, [PANK], Bombay Gin, Mom Egg Review, Denver Quarterly, Moonshot, Hotel Amerika, Cadillac Cicatrix, Puerto del Sol, Slipstream, Evergreen Chronicles,* and *Anthology of Georgia Poetry,* published by Negative Capability Press.

Patricia Powell

Patricia Powell is the author of *Me Dying Trial, A Small Gathering of Bones, The Pagoda,* and most recently *The Fullness of Everything.* Powell directs the MFA program at Mills College.

Your Own Heart pg. 200

adrienne maree

adrienne maree brown is a writer, science fiction scholar, social justice facilitator, doula, artist, auntie, and emergent strategist living in Detroit.

enclaves pg. 217

Kay Ulanday Barrett

A Campus Pride Hot List artist, 2013 Trans Justice Funding Project Panelist, and 2013 Trans 100 Honoree, Kay Ulanday Barrett is a poet, performer, and educator, navigating life as a disabled pin@y-amerikan transgender queer in the U.S. with struggle, resistance, and laughter. K. has featured on colleges & stages globally; Princeton University, UC Berkeley, Musee Pour Rire in Montreal, and The Chicago Historical Society. K's bold work continues to excite and challenge audiences. K. has facilitated workshops, presented keynotes, and contributed to panels with various social justice communities. Honors include: 18 Million Rising Filipino American History Month Hero 2013, Chicago's LGBTQ 30 under 30 awards, Finalist for The Gwendolyn Brooks Open-Mic Award, *Windy City Times* Pride Literary Poetry Prize. Their contributions are found in *Poor Magazine, Kicked Out Anthology, Trans Bodies/Trans Selves, Windy City Queer: Dispatches from the Third Coast, Make/Shift, Filipino American Psychology, Asian Americans For Progress, The Advocate,* and *Bitch Magazine.* K. turns art into action and is dedicated to remixing recipes. See their online swerve on twitter @ kulandaybarrett or his website.

kaybarrett.net

Brown Out Shouts! pg. 225

About the Editors

Helen Klonaris

Helen Klonaris is a Greek Bahamian writer living in the Bay Area, California, where she teaches creative writing and mythology at the Academy of Art University. Her work has appeared in numerous journals including *The Caribbean Writer, SX Salon, Tongues of the Ocean, Poui, ProudFlesh,* and *Calyx,* and several anthologies, including *Our Caribbean: A Gathering of Lesbian and Gay Writings from the Antilles* and *The Racial Imaginary: Writers on Race in the Life of the Mind.* Her story "Cowboy" was shortlisted in the 2014 Commonwealth Short Story Prize, and she has completed her debut collection of short stories *The Lovers.*

helenklonaris.com

Amir Rabiyah

Amir Rabiyah is a queer, disabled, and two-spirit writer of Lebanese, Syrian, Cherokee, and European ancestry. Amir has been published in *Mizna, Sukoon, The Feminist Wire, Bird's Thumb, Troubling the Line: Trans and Genderqueer Poetry and Poetics, Enizigam, Collective Brightness: LGBTIQ Poets on Faith, Religion and Spirituality,* and more. Amir currently lives in San Diego with their partner, and is working on completing a full length collection of poetry.

amirrabiyah.com

Acknowledgments

Amir Rabiyah:

I offer my sincere gratitude to the following people and organizations for their love and support, without you this book would not have been possible.

Thank you to Helen Klonaris, my fierce and fabulous co-editor. You are my sister in revolution, a dear friend and a wonderful co-editor. Without your vision, dedication and collaboration, this book would have not been possible. Thank you for your heart, your radical honesty and fierceness. I couldn't think of anyone else I'd rather work on this project with. I am honored to know you. Together, we are writing the walls down!

Thank you to A.J. Bryce and Trans-Genre Press. You believed in us when we were ready to move forward with this anthology. You are a wonderful publisher and human being. Thank you for all your hard work, your kindness and your passion.

Thank you to Riley for helping us with the final edits. You are a wizard.

Thank you to The Queer Cultural Center and Pam Peniston for accepting The Walls Project into the National Queer Arts Festival in 2010. We didn't know it then, but this was the inspiration for our anthology. Thank you to The African American Art and Culture Complex for opening your doors to us. Thanks to all of the artists and volunteers who participated in The Walls Project.

VONA/Voices: Writing Workshops for Writers of Color, I will probably be thanking you forever. You gave me shelter and listened to me when I thought no one would want to hear what I have to say. You have nurtured and inspired me as a writer. Without you, I do not know if I would have had the courage to stay on this writing path.

Shukran to Dr. Ibrahim (Baba) Farajejé for offering me a spiritual home and for your guidance. I have so much love and respect for you. I have truly appreciated all of our conversations about radical spirituality, inclusion, social justice, queerness, and chronic illness. You are the flyest Baba I've ever known.

Thank you to Shawna for supporting me as an artist and human being over the course of nearly a decade. I appreciate how much you have helped me grow and all you have taught me.

I send blessings and gratitude to Kin Folkz and Blackberri for bringing together such beautiful souls in Oakland at the open mic night and for welcoming me. I have so much respect for the two of you and how you cultivate community. Thank you for connecting me with some of the artists who ended up in these pages and for inspiring me to keep on going.

To my partner Julia Ris, thank you for being on this path with me. Thank you for supporting me through all of my hardships, my chronic illnesses, and creative life. Thank you for being patient through the process of this anthology, the long hours, and the emotional ups and downs. You are a brilliant and incredible partner and I love you deeply.

To all of the contributors, words cannot express my gratitude. Thank you for sharing your words and art with me, for your courage, your beauty and the gift of your energies in these pages.

Thank you to all the donors and people who donated to our fundraising campaign. You rock. You have helped our book get out in the world and have support Trans-Genre Press in remaining sustainable.

Thank you to all my friends and chosen family who have supported me over the years, especially through the process of this anthology. Thank you for your sweet messages of comfort, for bringing me food and helping me with tasks when I was too sick and bedridden. You helped me stay alive and more importantly offered care when I needed it most. I love you all. Thank you to my brother, for helping me stay housed. Thank you to my sweet support animals, Soli and Foxxxy, for being by my side in sickness and health and for stepping on my computer when I was writing important things.

Finally, gratitude to the Creator, the Universe, the One, that which contains multitudes, everything, the Source, thank you for giving me the opportunity to be an artist and to be alive.

Helen Klonaris:

There are many without whom this anthology would not have been possible:

First and foremost, I want to say thank you to my friend, my collaborator, my soul brother Amir Rabiyah for saying yes to this journey even before we conceived of it. Our friendship, the kindred spirit I feel with you, the deep respect I have for who you are in the world, your compassion and insight, your commitment to a sacred revolution and the way you live it everyday – these are the ground out of which *Writing the Walls Down* emerged. I am so proud to be your co-conspirator in editing this anthology!

A.J. Bryce, from the moment you said yes to the query letter Amir and I sent to you one day in October, from a tiny coffee shop off 18th Street in Oakland, you have been a steady source of confidence in our vision and how to bring it into the world. Your vision for Trans-Genre Press is deeply inspiring and I thank you for believing in *Writing the Walls Down* and working with us tirelessly to make it real.

To my partner in love and life, Patricia Powell, thank you for being my ally, my inspiratrice, my deep support, my witness; your patience and love and belief in my writing and creative work make worlds possible.

To my friend Prajna Choudury, I thank you for conversations, your compassion and visionary spirit, your integrity of heart and mind. Your commitment to our friendship has been a sustaining fire in my life.

To The Rainbow Alliance of the Bahamas, you were there at the beginning, in our living rooms and on the streets, speaking and scheming and imagining. Together we knew we could write down, talk down, dance down, love down the walls that kept us from being ourselves. Your courage, your belief in 'circles that included everyone', made it possible to see a world in which our lives could be. Thank you.

To Pam Peniston and the Queer Cultural Center where The Walls Project had its debut; to the African American Art and Culture Complex that hosted us, and all the volunteers and performers and artists who participated and supported us, thank you. You were the first convergence.

To Arnold Thomas, many years ago you asked, "What would happen if you spill the beans?" This anthology is one answer. Your wisdom, your connection to Spirit, your witness inspired me to follow the serpentine path of my most true self; I will be forever grateful.

To Mary and Jimmy Klonaris, you have walked with me down this road, allowing yourselves to be challenged, but you kept on walking, even when you didn't know where we would end up. I am grateful to you beyond words.

To Tanya Klonaris Azevedo, Tina Klonaris Robinson, and Maria Govan, your love and support of me through all the years has been a gift like no other. You are my allies, my angels, my protectors, my fierce and wise heroines. My gratitude is bottomless.

To our contributors, thank you for trusting us with your words and visions; they have moved me beyond measure. My wide and deep thanks.

Riley, your eyes on these words made all the difference! Thank you.

To all who donated towards the publication of this book, thank you, thank you, thank you.

And to the Sacred alive in all things, thank you for life, thank you for connection, thank you for cracks in walls and seedling womantongue trees growing rebellions from them.

Thank You

Also from Trans-Genre Press:

Seasonal Velocities by Ryka Aoki

 *Seasonal Velocities* invites the reader on a fragile and furious journey along the highways and skyways of discovery, retribution, and resolve. Through her poetry, essays, stories, and performances, award-winning writer Ryka Aoki has consistently challenged, informed, and enthralled queer audiences across the United States.

Queer Heartache by Kit Yan (forthcoming)

 *Queer Heartache* follows Kit from his childhood in Hawaii as a poor child of immigrants, to Kit's move to the continental U.S. and his experiences with hate crimes, bathrooms, and gender. In this book, we hear about the importance and complications of family for Kit as a queer, transgender, polyamorous, sexual person. *Queer Heartache* tackles the shortcomings of the medical and social services systems in America, and ultimately seeks to find a story within all of these struggles. *Queer Heartache* is the hurt and hope in these everyday stories.

Trans-Genre Press is a radical, independently run press committed to supporting the voices of marginalized people, specifically those who identify as Transgender/Gender Variant and our collaborative allies.

For more information, visit Trans-Genre.net

CPSIA information can be obtained at www.ICGtesting.com
Printed in the USA
BVOW11s2155280915

419688BV00002B/1/P